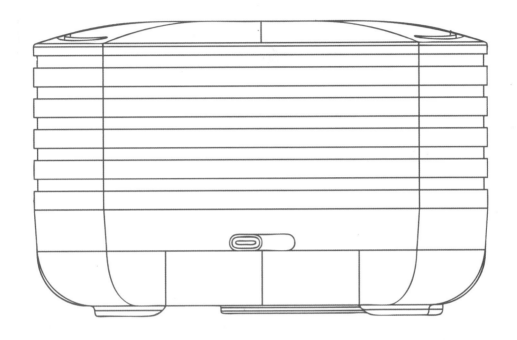

Dehydrating
at Home

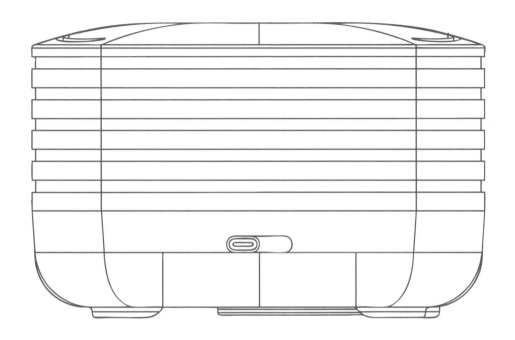

Dehydrating at Home

Michelle Keogh
with an introduction by
Karielyn Tillman

**Getting the best from your dehydrator,
from fruit leathers to meat jerkies**

FIREFLY BOOKS

A FIREFLY BOOK

Published by Firefly Books Ltd. 2015

First printing

Publisher Cataloging-in-Publication Data (U.S.)

Keogh, Michelle.
    Dehydrating at home : getting the best from your dehydrator, from fruit leathers to meat jerkies / Michelle Keogh ; Paul Nelson, photographer.
[192] pages : photographs (some color) ; cm.
Includes index.
Summary: "A guide to dehydrating. Includes chapters on: Food prep & storage, fruit, vegetables, leathers, jerky, nuts & seeds, crackers & flatbreads, herbs, breakfast, entrées, desserts, cooked meals, pet treats and household uses." – from Publisher.
ISBN-13: 978-1-77085-586-1 (pbk.)
1. Food – Drying. 2. Cooking (Dried foods). 3. Dried foods. I. Nelson, Paul. II. Title.
641.44 dc23   TX609.K464 2015

Library and Archives Canada Cataloguing in Publication

Keogh, Michelle, author
    Dehydrating at home : getting the best from your dehydrator, from fruit leathers to meat jerkies / Michelle Keogh, author ; Paul Nelson, photographer.
Includes index.
ISBN 978-1-77085-586-1 (pbk.)
    1. Food—Drying. 2. Cooking (Dried foods). 3. Dried foods. I. Title.
TX609.K46 2015   641.4'4   C2015-901629-0

Published in the United States by
Firefly Books (U.S.) Inc.
P.O. Box 1338, Ellicott Station
Buffalo, New York 14205

Published in Canada by
Firefly Books Ltd.
50 Staples Avenue, Unit 1
Richmond Hill, Ontario L4B 0A7

Printed in China by Shanghai Offset Printing Products Ltd.

Conceived, designed, and produced by
Quintet Publishing
Project Editor: Katherine Stathers
Publishing Assistant: Alice Sambrook
Designer: Luke Herriott
Photographer: Paul Nelson
Art Director: Michael Charles
Editorial Director: Alana Smythe
Publisher: Mark Searle

Contents

Introduction

The art of dehydrating foods dates back to ancient times when the sun and wind were used to preserve and save produce for the winter months.

Today, the dehydrator has become a healthy addition to the modern kitchen with many benefits and uses.

I have owned my dehydrator for almost eight years and I use it for everything from drying soaked nuts and seeds, to making creative snacks and treats, to just drying tasty seasonal fruits so I can enjoy them all year round.

One of my favorites is strawberries. During strawberry season, I like to stock up and will buy one or two flats of strawberries. I'll bring them home, prep them, load up my dehydrator and then we get to enjoy dried strawberries long after strawberry season is over.

I also love making healthy snacks like fruit roll-ups, crackers and chips for my two young boys. This way I have control over the quality of ingredients used — no preservatives, or artificial colors and flavorings. The boys prefer them to store-bought snacks because they taste better, and I prefer it because they're not packed with empty calories and little nutrition.

Another great benefit of dehydrating, of course, is that it's so economical compared with buying pre-packaged dried snacks or herbs in the store.

But the number one reason I use my dehydrator over other appliances in my kitchen is for the health benefits. The human body is made up of living cells that need living "live" food to maintain optimal health and prevent disease. Every day we have the choice to eat living "live" food or cooked "dead" food. When you use a dehydrator and dehydrate your foods under 118°F (47°C), they remain "live" and retain the majority of their nutrients, as opposed to literally cooking the life out of them.

This book will take you through the process for dehydrating each type of food with helpful hints and delicious recipes. Each chapter focuses on a different skill, from drying simple fruits and vegetables to making fruit leathers, creating tasty jerky, dehydrating nuts and seeds, creating delicious raw meals and sweets, and even making healthy treats for your pets. Once you have the hang of a particular skill, feel free to experiment with different ingredients and flavors; you'll find dehydrating a very forgiving method of preparing food, once you've mastered the basics.

Karielyn Tillman
thehealthyfamilyandhome.com

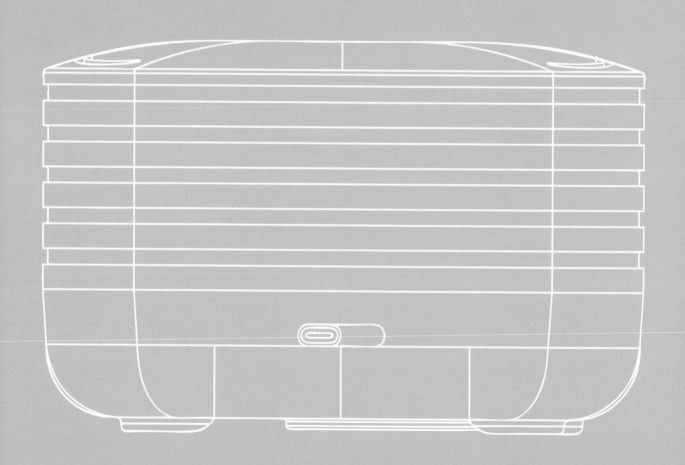

Chapter One:
Basics

This chapter tells you everything you need to know about dehydrating, from buying a dehydrator that's right for you, to proper food preparation and storage. It also gives you helpful information about the factors that might affect drying times and the tools you'll need for the job.

The Basics of Dehydrating

How a Food Dehydrator Works its Magic

Dehydrating food really is the simplest process; essentially, all you are doing is removing the moisture from food. In ancient times, this would have been done by leaving the food out in a sunny, breezy spot, allowing nature to do the work for you. Modern dehydrators remove the moisture from food by a continuous circulation of thermostatically controlled warm air. The operational cost of a dehydrator is quite low, making it a viable alternative when compared with traditional canning or freezing methods to preserve food.

What Makes a Good Dehydrator?

Dehydrators are fairly simple machines, but there are variations in design and size. Some are circular and have the heating and fan units in the bottom of the machine, with shelves that stack one on top of the other and a lid on top. Others are square, with the heating and fan coming from the rear of the unit, tray shelves that slide in and out and a door on the front.

The circular/stackable machines are generally more compact and less expensive, but there is only one shelf height and everything you make needs to fit onto a ring-shaped surface. This means you can't use it for making yogurt, raising bread or anything else that has some height. The advantage of a stackable dehydrator is that you can add or remove shelves to the unit, giving you a bit more versatility in size. The disadvantage

can be that the air doesn't circulate evenly, meaning you may need to rotate the shelves while drying.

Square/shelf tray machines can be a lot bulkier, but the shelving heights are usually adjustable, meaning you can use the dehydrator for taller/bigger items and spread whatever you are making over a larger surface area. Square dehydrators come in a variety of sizes — five trays, nine trays, ten trays and so on. While you can remove shelves from these dehydrators, the unit will still be the same size, and you can't add extra shelves as you can with a stackable model.

In general, the more you spend, the better features such as temperature control and timers may be, allowing for greater accuracy.

Soaking Times for Nuts and Seeds

Ingredient	Soaking Time	Drying Time
Almond	8–12 hours	12–24 hours
Brazil nut	Do not soak	
Buckwheat	15 minutes	8–12 hours
Cashew	2–3 hours	12–24 hours
Chia seed	2–3 hours	
Flaxseed	2–3 hours	8–12 hours
Hazelnut	8–10 hours	12–24 hours
Macadamia	Do not soak	
Pecan	4–6 hours	12–24 hours
Pepita	8 hours	8–12 hours
Pine nut	Do not soak	
Pistachio	Do not soak	
Sunflower seed	2–4 hours	8–12 hours
Walnut	4–6 hours	12–24 hours

Preparing Food for Dehydration

When slicing foods for dehydration, it is important to slice to a uniform thickness to avoid uneven drying. Using a mandolin or slicer is by far the best way to do this. Partially freezing meats can assist with even slicing, as it will be firmer and easier to cut.

Fresh and lean cuts of meat are best for dehydrating. Avoid anything too fatty, as it will spoil easily and could cause illness.

To maintain the "live" nature of foods, the temperature should not go above 118°F (47°C). However, I would recommend that you begin drying at the highest temperature possible (155°F (68°C)) for the first two to three hours then turn it down to the desired temperature — usually 115°F (46°C) — for the remaining time. During those first three hours the food temperature will not exceed 118°F (47°C) because of the high moisture content of the food and because the air temperature takes some time to rise. Drying raw foods in this fashion cuts the drying time by many hours and greatly lowers the potential for food spoilage and bacteria growth.

Herbs and spices retain their colors and flavors best at lower temperatures: between 95°F (35°C) and 115°F (46°C). They should be well washed and patted dry before dehydrating. Keep the leaves of herbs attached to the stems, otherwise they may blow everywhere during dehydrating.

Raw nuts and seeds should be dried between 115°F (46°C) and 125°F (52°C), and can be dried as they are, or with spices and seasonings added. There is some belief that soaking nuts and seeds before drying them increases their digestibility and activates their full nutrient potential (see chart on left for soaking and drying times). Make sure nuts and seeds have dried completely to avoid mold growth during storage.

Vegetables dry best at 125°F (52°C) and should be well washed or peeled before drying. Some vegetables, particularly root varieties such as potatoes and beets, are better steamed or blanched first. To do this, simply boil or steam the item for three to four minutes before placing it into iced water to cool, then slicing and drying as normal.

Fruits can be dried at slightly higher temperatures than vegetables, 135°F (57°C), and should be prepared and stored in the same way. Some fruits — such as the tougher skinned ones: grapes, cranberries and plums — may benefit from being blanched for a minute or two in order to "craze" the skin, allowing moisture to escape more easily during drying.

Leathers and roll-ups can be dried at the same temperature as fruit. Fruits don't necessarily need to be cooked before pureeing, and leaving the skins on, where possible, will add to the fiber and nutrient content. For wetter fruits such as berries and pineapple, adding a banana or two to the puree can help thicken the mixture and give a thicker, chewier fruit leather. Yogurt can be added to fruit for fruit leathers, or dehydrated on its own for a taffy-like treat. Likewise, nut butters can be added to fruit leathers for different flavors and textures, as can dried coconut or chopped nuts. Leathers can also be made from steamed and pureed vegetables, which can then be eaten as snacks or rehydrated to form the basis of soups, stews and sauces. Vegetable leathers should be dried at 125°F (52°C).

When making jerky, choose fresh, lean cuts of meat. The best drying temperature for meat is 155°F (68°C) because of the potential for spoilage or illness caused by improperly prepared meat. The best kinds of meat to use are beef, pork, game or fish. All meats, particularly poultry and fish, should be extremely fresh to prevent it spoiling before it has dried fully. Oily fish should be used with caution, as there is no way to trim the fat away and it can spoil rapidly.

Meat will preserve better if it has been cured or brined before drying. Dry cures are generally composed of salt and seasonings, applied evenly to the meat then left in the refrigerator for 6 to 12 hours or overnight. Brines or marinades are salt and seasonings combined with water, then layered with the meat, covering it completely and leaving it in the refrigerator for 6 to 12 hours or overnight. Once the jerky has properly dried it should crack, but not break, when bent.

It is important to select the right temperature for the food you are drying. If the temperature is too high, the food will "case harden," meaning it will feel dry on the outside but still be too moist on the inside. When the temperature is too low, food will take far longer to dry, meaning more electricity is used and the food has a higher risk of spoiling.

TOP TIP

Prevent fruits such as apples and pears oxidizing (turning brown) by dipping them in one of the following solutions after slicing but before dehydrating:

Citric acid/ascorbic acid dip — Mix 2 tablespoons (30 ml) of citric acid to 1 quart (1.1 l) of water and soak your fruit for two minutes. Rinse and drain thoroughly.

Fruit juice dip — Add 1 cup (240 ml) of juice to 1 quart (1.1 l) of water and soak prepared fruit for 10 minutes, rinse and drain thoroughly, and dehydrate as normal. Using citrus juices may add a flavor to your food.

Honey dip — Use 1 cup (240 ml) of honey dissolved in 3 cups (720 ml) of warm water to dip prepared fruit and then drain well before dehydrating. Using honey will add considerable sweetness to your food and is probably best reserved for tart fruits such as rhubarb and cranberries.

Variables that Can Affect Drying Times

Drying times are never exact and the following variables can affect them:

- **Atmospheric humidity:** the higher the moisture content in the air, the longer your food will take to dry, regardless of the actual air temperature.

- **Moisture and sugar content:** the water content of the food you are drying is a major factor in drying times, as is the sugar content because sugars attract water. The water content of fruits and vegetables can vary due to ripeness, rainfall and other environmental factors.

- **Method of preparation:** making sure your food is sliced uniformly and not too thickly goes a long way towards ensuring your food dries evenly and quickly. Blanching or steaming food where appropriate will also reduce drying times.

- **Types of dehydrator:** dehydrators with back-mounted heating and fan units are generally quicker than those with top- or bottom-mounted fans, as the air can circulate more freely. Rotating the trays during drying can make a huge difference when solving this problem.

- **Amount of food:** overloading your dehydrator trays will mean that the air cannot circulate properly and dry your food efficiently. The more food you have in your dehydrator, the longer items will take to dry.

The drying times given with these recipes vary greatly and should only be used as a guide. Check your dehydrating items every few hours and remove them once they reach the desired level of dryness. If you are unsure as to whether an item is completely dry, pop it into an airtight bag for a few minutes: if water droplets form inside the bag, it needs longer to dry. With experience you will become adept at knowing when your food is dry. Until then, it is best to dry food for longer if you are unsure. You won't spoil food by over drying it.

Food Storage

Completely dried foods with a low fat content should be stored in airtight containers or bags that are free of moisture in a cool dark place. Glass jars with tight-fitting lids, zip-lock bags, vacuum/heat-sealable bags and airtight plastic containers are the best storage options. Food-safe metal tins, such as cookie tins, can be used for storing individually bagged items.

Semi-dried foods, or dried foods that have a high fat content — these include nuts, bread, tomatoes and some desserts — should be stored in airtight containers in the refrigerator or freezer. The reason for this is the fat or moisture content of these foods makes them prone to spoilage or going rancid.

If moisture beads form inside a storage container, the food has not dried properly and needs to continue drying in the dehydrator.

Herbs and spices are best stored away from direct sunlight to prevent the colors and flavors from deteriorating.

How to Rehydrate Food

While dehydrated foods can easily be incorporated into your everyday life, with snacks such as dried fruit, veggie crackers and raw meals, there may be times you wish to reconstitute the food you have dried. If foods have been dried properly to start with, they will rehydrate well, returning to almost the same size and appearance as they were when fresh. There are a few methods you can try for reconstituting food, including soaking in water or juice, using a steamer, placing food into boiling water or cooking. It is important not to add anything to the food, such as salt, sugar or spices, in the first five minutes of reconstituting, as these can hinder the absorption of liquids.

- **Soaking:** place the dried food into a shallow pan, cover with liquid and allow the food one to two hours to rehydrate. If leaving the food overnight, store it in the refrigerator.
- **Steaming:** place the food into the top half of a double boiler or into an electric steamer and steam the food until it has rehydrated.
- **Boiling water:** to reconstitute dried fruits and vegetables, place 1 cup (240 ml) of vegetables into 1 cup (240 ml) of boiling water and soak for five to 20 minutes. Or place 1 cup (240 ml) of fruit and 1 cup (240 ml) of water into a pan and simmer until the fruit is tender.
- **Cooking:** you can add dried foods directly to the dish you are cooking using the ratios of 1 part dried food and 1 part water, and simmer gently for one to 15 minutes to rehydrate.

Other Ways You Can Use Your Dehydrator

Re-crisp food that has gone stale and soft, such as crackers, chips, cookies or cereals.

Create an environment with a steady temperature, for example when you're making cheese, bread, yogurt or other cultures and ferments.

Turn excess stock or soup into powder for easy storage. Reduce it until it's thick and viscous first.

Make crispy breadcrumbs by completely drying out any stale bread, then popping it into your food processor or blender to process it into crumbs.

Evenly dry out decorative ornaments such as those made from cinnamon or salt dough to avoid the risk of burning.

Beyond the Box: Other Tools You Might Need

Mandolin: this is a wonderful piece of kitchen equipment, extremely useful for slicing food evenly and cutting it into matchsticks. Most have at least two thickness settings for slicing, meaning you can choose the one that suits you best. Mandolins are fantastic for foods that are difficult to slice evenly by hand, such as hard fruits, root vegetables and other vegetables such as squash, zucchini, eggplant and pumpkin.

Food processor: a food processor is indispensable in the kitchen if you want to create ground nuts, fruit purees for fruit leather, or herb, spice or vegetable powders. Some also have slicing and grating attachments that can be very useful, too.

Blender: a good-quality blender can be used in the same way as a food processor, minus the slicing and grating options.

Slicer: an electric slicer can be very handy if you are making a lot of sliced goods, such as jerky and vegetable chips.

Peeler: a vegetable peeler is a great preparation tool for peeling fruits and vegetables, but also for making very fine slices or removing zest from citrus fruits.

Spatula: a spatula or palette knife is the perfect tool for spreading out any wet mixtures for dehydrating, such as fruit leather, raw crackers, raw crêpes and breads.

Knives: good-quality, sharp knives are essential in any kitchen, but especially when preparing food for dehydrating. With practice you will become adept at slicing foods to even thicknesses, and preparing them for drying.

Cookie scoop: a spring-release cookie or ice-cream scoop is such a fantastic tool to have in your kitchen. It allows you to make perfectly portioned and shaped cookies and bites easily. Simply scoop your mixture up, push it in firmly and press the lever to release it onto the tray.

Cherry pitter: while not essential, a cherry pitter is handy for drying large amounts of cherries.

Zester: also not essential, but very useful if you wish to dry large amounts of citrus zest.

Essential equipment for dehydrating at home: food processor, mandolin, zester, sharp knife, palate knife, cookie scoop, corer and peeler.

Can You Use an Oven to Dehydrate Food?

Dehydrators have become so popular because they are more energy-efficient than an oven, and dry food more uniformly. However, for many of the recipes in this book, you could use an oven and experiment with drying times which will vary considerably. Prepare the food in the same way as for the dehydrator and set the oven temperature to 140°F (60°C). Leave the oven door slightly open to allow the moisture to escape and turn the baking sheets around regularly to dry the food evenly.

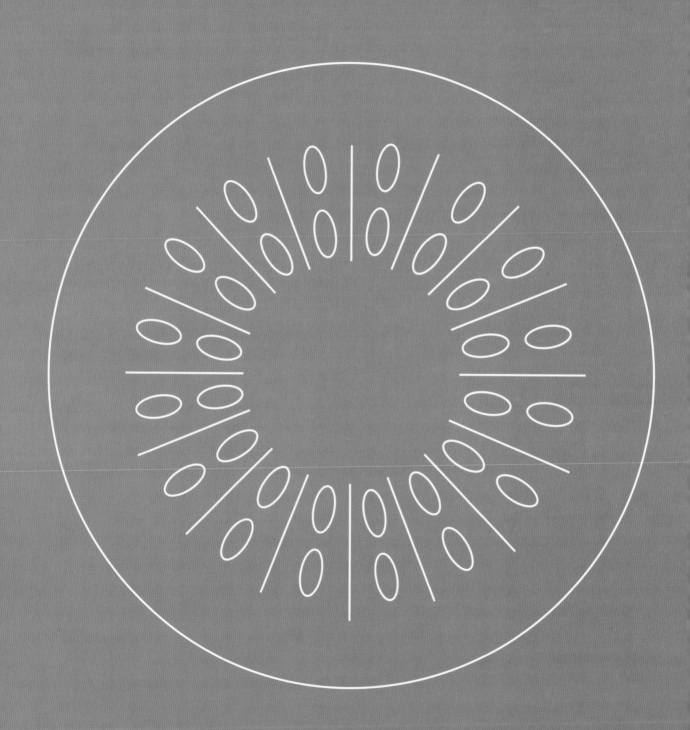

Chapter Two:
Fruits

This chapter includes quick and easy recipes for getting started as well as compelling ideas for the more adventurous reader, such as Double-dehydrated Coconut Vanilla Bananas — which are dehydrated bananas, rehydrated in coconut milk and dehydrated again. Fruits will dry best at 135°F (57°C). If you want an end product that is still technically raw, dry fruits at 115°F (46°C) or lower, and extend the drying times.

▲ **Yield:** 4–8 servings

● **Prep time:** 10–15 minutes

〰 **Drying time:** 7–15 hours

Cinnamon Apple Rings

Ingredients:

- *4 medium apples*
- *Cinnamon sugar, to taste*

If you are worried about your apples going brown, dip them in a solution of 2 cups (480 ml) water and 2 tablespoons (30 ml) lemon juice right after they have been sliced.

Method:

1. Wash and core the apples using an apple corer.

2. Slice the apples using a mandolin set to ¼ inch (5 mm) thick.

3. Arrange the slices on a dehydrator tray. Avoid overcrowding the slices because air needs to circulate around them.

4. Sprinkle lightly with cinnamon sugar, or to taste.

5. Dry at 135°F (57°C) for 7 to 15 hours, rotating the trays a few times during dehydrating, until dry and pliable. Store in an airtight container at room temperature.

- **Yield:** Varies
- **Prep time:** Variable
- **Drying time:** 20–28 hours

- **Yield:** Varies
- **Prep time:** Variable
- **Drying time:** 20–28 hours

Plums (Prunes)

Ingredients:

- *Enough plums to fill your dehydrator*

This is a wonderful way to use up a variety of plums at the season's peak. Choose ripe fruit; small blemishes and bruises won't affect the finished product. Prunes make a delicious snack as they come, or try rehydrating them in flavored tea for a treat.

Method:

1. Prepare the fruit by cutting along its vertical crease. Twist each half in opposite directions to separate them from the pit. Discard the pit.

2. Arrange the halves skin-side down on the dehydrator trays. Avoid overcrowding because air needs to circulate around them.

3. Dry at 135°F (57°C) for 20 to 28 hours, rotating the trays a few times during dehydrating, until leathery. Store in an airtight container at room temperature.

Grapes (Raisins)

Ingredients:

- *Enough grapes to fill your dehydrator*

Use any variety of ripe grapes you prefer, seedless are best for ease of eating. Muscatels dried in small bunches make a wonderful addition to a cheese board.

Method:

1. Prepare the fruit by washing and removing the grapes from the stem (unless drying as a bunch).

2. Arrange on the dehydrator trays. Avoid overcrowding because air needs to circulate around them.

3. Dry at 135°F (57°C) for 20 to 28 hours, rotating the trays a few times during dehydrating, until dry and pliable. Store in an airtight container at room temperature.

- **Yield:** Varies
- **Prep time:** Variable
- **Drying time:** 12–20 hours

- **Yield:** Varies
- **Prep time:** Variable
- **Drying time:** 8–14 hours

Cherries

Ingredients:

- *Enough cherries to fill your dehydrator*

Cherries have such a short season; this is a great way to preserve them to eat throughout the year. You can use them in the same way you would raisins, for a delicious change in many recipes.

Method:

1. Remove the stems and pits from the cherries using a cherry pitter.

2. Arrange the cherries on the dehydrator trays. Avoid overcrowding because air needs to circulate around them.

3. Dry at 135°F (57°C) for 12 to 20 hours, rotating the trays a few times during dehydrating, until sticky and leathery. Store in an airtight container at room temperature.

Mango

Ingredients:

- *Enough mangoes to fill your dehydrator*

Mangoes keep their beautiful color when dried, and the flavor intensifies greatly, making them sweet, chewy and delicious. They make a fantastic snack, and can also be used to add a burst of flavor and color to many sweet and savory dishes.

Method:

1. Prepare the fruit by cutting the two cheeks off either side of the pit. Peel the cheeks using a sharp knife.

2. Cut the cheeks into ¼-inch (5 mm) slices and arrange on the dehydrator trays. Avoid overcrowding because air needs to circulate around them.

3. Dry at 135°F (57°C) for 8 to 14 hours, rotating the trays a few times during dehydrating, until leathery. Store in an airtight container at room temperature.

- **Yield:** 4–8 servings
- **Prep time:** 15–20 minutes
- **Drying time:** 8–12 hours

Ingredients:

- 1 bunch (5–6 stalks) rhubarb, leaves removed
- ¼ cup (60 ml) maple syrup

Maple Syrup Dipped Rhubarb

These tangy, sweet-and-sour treats are delicious in trail mix, or added to salads. Be sure to discard the poisonous rhubarb leaves away from children and pets.

Method:

1. Prepare the fruit by cutting it into 1-inch (2.5 cm) pieces.

2. Place the rhubarb pieces into a medium mixing bowl, add the maple syrup and toss well, until all the rhubarb is evenly coated with maple syrup.

3. Spread the rhubarb pieces onto dehydrator trays lined with non-stick sheets or baking parchment. Avoid overcrowding because air needs to circulate around them.

4. Drizzle any remaining maple syrup from the bowl over the rhubarb.

5. Dry at 135°F (57°C) for 8 to 12 hours, rotating the trays a few times during dehydrating, until sticky and leathery. Store in an airtight container at room temperature.

- ⚠ **Yield:** Varies
- 🕐 **Prep time:** Variable
- 〰 **Drying time:** 12–20 hours

- ⚠ **Yield:** Varies
- 🕐 **Prep time:** Variable
- 〰 **Drying time:** 8–14 hours

Pineapple

Ingredients:

- *Enough pineapple to fill your dehydrator*

For a different variation on the recipe below, very fine slices of peeled pineapple with the core left in can be dried and used as edible decorations on cakes and desserts; they look just like lovely yellow flowers.

Method:

1. Peel and core the pineapple, and remove the fibrous eyes using a sharp knife.

2. Cut the pineapple into ½-inch (1 cm) rings and arrange on the dehydrator trays. Avoid overcrowding because air needs to circulate around them.

3. Dry at 135°F (57°C) for 12 to 20 hours, rotating the trays a few times during dehydrating, until dry and pliable. Store in an airtight container at room temperature.

Kiwi

Ingredients:

- *Enough kiwis to fill your dehydrator*

Drying kiwi fruit is a fantastic way to have this seasonal fruit available all year round. They become tart and chewy when dried, a wonderful addition to a dried fruit mix, muesli and desserts.

Method:

1. Prepare the fruit by peeling and slicing into ¼-inch (5 mm) rounds using a sharp knife.

2. Arrange the slices on the dehydrator trays. Avoid overcrowding because air needs to circulate around them.

3. Dry at 135°F (57°C) for 8 to 14 hours, rotating the trays a few times during dehydrating, until leathery. Store in an airtight container at room temperature.

Amaretto Dipped Apricots

⚠ **Yield:** 20–24 halves

🕐 **Prep time:** 1 hour 15 minutes

♨ **Drying time:** 20–28 hours

Apricots are another fruit to take advantage of while they're in season! Choose ripe, sweet fruit; slight blemishes will not affect the final product. These apricots have been soaked in amaretto for a decadent treat, but apricots are also delightful dried as they are.

Ingredients:

- 1 lb (450 g) apricots
- 2 tbsp (25 g) granulated sugar
- ¼ cup (60 ml) amaretto

Method:

1. Prepare the fruit by cutting along its vertical crease. Twist each half in opposite directions to separate them from the pit. Discard the pit.

2. Place the apricots skin side down into a large mixing bowl, sprinkle the granulated sugar over them, followed by the amaretto. Allow the fruit to macerate for 1 hour, tossing gently from time to time.

3. Arrange the apricots skin-side down onto dehydrator trays lined with non-stick sheets or baking parchment. Avoid overcrowding because air needs to circulate around them.

4. Spoon some of the remaining amaretto mixture over them.

5. Dry at 135°F (57°C) for 20 to 28 hours, rotating the trays a few times during dehydrating, until sticky and leathery. Store in an airtight container at room temperature.

Watermelon Chips with Lime

Ingredients:

- 1 small, seedless watermelon
- 4 limes

These watermelon "chips" make a sweet, tangy snack. For best results, use a watermelon that is as ripe as possible and, for ease of eating, seedless.

Method:

1. Prepare the fruit by cutting it into quarters, then cutting off the peel using a sharp knife. Cut the quarters into ½-inch (1 cm) slices and place them into a large bowl.

2. Zest and juice the limes, and sprinkle both over the watermelon slices. Gently toss the watermelon in the lime.

3. Arrange the watermelon slices on the dehydrator trays. Avoid overcrowding because air needs to circulate around them.

4. Dry at 135°F (57°C) for 20 to 28 hours, rotating the trays a few times during dehydrating, until dry and pliable. Store in an airtight container at room temperature.

Double-dehydrated Coconut Vanilla Bananas

Ingredients:

- 4 large, ripe bananas
- I cup (240 ml) coconut milk
- 2 tsp (10 ml) vanilla extract

These double-dehydrated bananas taste like creamy coconut caramels — delicious! Take care when handling the rehydrated bananas after they have been soaked in the coconut milk, as they become a little delicate.

Method:

I. Prepare the fruit by peeling and slicing into ¼-inch (5 mm) rounds using a sharp knife.

2. Arrange the slices on the dehydrator trays. Avoid overcrowding because air needs to circulate around them.

3. Dry at 135°F (57°C) for 4 to 8 hours, rotating the trays a few times during dehydrating.

4. Once the bananas are dry and leathery, remove them from the dehydrator.

5. Place the coconut milk and vanilla extract into a medium saucepan, place it over a medium-high heat and bring it to a simmer.

6. Remove the coconut milk from the heat and add the dried bananas to the saucepan; stir until all the bananas are covered in coconut milk.

7. Allow the bananas to soak until they have become soft and rehydrated, about 30 minutes.

8. Drain away the excess coconut milk and arrange the banana slices on the dehydrator trays. Avoid overcrowding because air needs to circulate around them.

9. Dry at 135°F (57°C) for a further 8 to 12 hours, rotating the trays a few times during drying, until dry and leathery.

10. Store in an airtight container in the refrigerator.

Double-dehydrated Balsamic Strawberries

Yield: 4–8 servings

Prep time: 3 hours 20 minutes

Drying time: 16–26 hours

Ingredients:

- 1 lb (450 g) strawberries
- ½ cup (120 ml) balsamic vinegar
- ½ cup (120 ml) water
- ¼ cup (50 g) brown sugar, lightly packed

Balsamic vinegar and strawberries are a match made in heaven. Be sure to choose very ripe strawberries; a few small blemishes will not affect the final product. These are a great addition to salads, cheese boards and desserts.

Method:

1. Prepare the fruit by washing and removing the tops using a sharp knife.

2. Cut the strawberries in half from top to bottom.

3. Arrange the halves on the dehydrator trays. Avoid overcrowding because air needs to circulate around them.

4. Dry at 135°F (57°C) for 8 to 14 hours, rotating the trays a few times during dehydrating.

5. Once the strawberries are dry and leathery, remove them from the dehydrator.

6. Place the balsamic vinegar, water and brown sugar into a medium saucepan, place it over a medium-high heat and bring it to the boil, stirring to dissolve the sugar.

7. Remove the balsamic mixture from the heat and add the dried strawberries to the saucepan.

8. Allow the strawberries to soak in the balsamic mixture until they have become soft and rehydrated, around 3 hours.

9. Drain away the excess balsamic and arrange the strawberries on the dehydrator trays. Avoid overcrowding because air needs to circulate around them.

10. Dry at 135°F (57°C) for a further 8 to 12 hours, rotating the trays a few times during drying, until sticky and leathery.

11. Store in an airtight container in the refrigerator.

Chapter Three:
Vegetables

This chapter includes savory snacks as well as recipes for preserving your harvest successfully for months, if not years, to come. Vegetables will dry best at 135°F (57°C). If you want an end product that is still technically raw, dry vegetables at 105°F (40°C) and extend the drying times.

⚠ **Yield:** Varies

🕐 **Prep time:** Variable

〰 **Drying time:** 6–8 hours

⚠ **Yield:** Varies

🕐 **Prep time:** Variable

〰 **Drying time:** 10–18 hours

Radishes

Ingredients:

- *Enough radishes to fill your dehydrator*

Crisp, dried radishes can be eaten as a tasty snack, or crumbled over salads. They can also be ground into a powder and added to dips and sauces for a peppery kick.

Method:

1. Prepare the radishes by trimming the tails and slicing them into ¼-inch (5 mm) slices.

2. Arrange the slices on the dehydrator trays. Avoid overcrowding because air needs to circulate around them.

3. Dry at 125°F (52°C) for 6 to 8 hours, rotating the trays a few times during dehydrating, until crisp. Store in an airtight container at room temperature.

Tomatoes

Ingredients:

- *Enough tomatoes to fill your dehydrator*

The tomatoes can be sprinkled with some herbs and salt before drying, for extra flavor. For semi-dried tomatoes, take them out of the dehydrator when they are dry to touch but still quite soft, and store in a jar of olive oil in the refrigerator.

Method:

1. Prepare the tomatoes by removing the cores and slicing them into ½-inch (1 cm) slices or wedges.

2. Arrange the tomatoes skin-side down (for wedges) on the dehydrator trays. Avoid overcrowding because air needs to circulate around them.

3. Dry at 125°F (52°C) for 10 to 18 hours, rotating the trays a few times during dehydrating, until dry and pliable. Store in an airtight container at room temperature.

Kale Chips

▲ **Yield:** 2–4 servings

● **Prep time:** 15–20 minutes

♨ **Drying time:** 3–7 hours

Ingredients:

- *1 large bunch of kale*
- *2 tbsp (30 ml) nutritional yeast*
- *2 tbsp (30 ml) apple cider vinegar*
- *¼ cup (60 ml) olive oil*
- *1 tsp (3 g) onion and garlic powder (see recipe on page 117)*
- *½ tsp (2 g) salt*

A deliciously crunchy, healthy snack; the flavor combinations are endless. Try adding chili powder for a kick, or finely grated parmesan for a cheesy treat. Kale chips are best consumed within a week of making, as they begin to go soft.

Method:

1. Prepare the kale by removing the leaves from the stems. Tear the leaves into roughly 2-inch (5 cm) pieces and place them into a large mixing bowl.

2. In a smaller bowl, mix together the nutritional yeast, apple cider vinegar, olive oil, onion and garlic powder, and salt. Mix well. Add this mixture to the kale and massage it into the leaves until they are all well coated.

3. Arrange the kale onto the dehydrator sheets in single layer; avoid overcrowding because air needs to circulate around them.

4. Dry at 125°F (52°C) for 3 to 7 hours, rotating the trays a few times during dehydrating, until crisp. Store in an airtight container at room temperature.

Tamari Carrots

⊿ **Yield:** 4 servings

◐ **Prep time:** 15–20 minutes

≋ **Drying time:** 6–10 hours

These vibrantly colored and delicious snacks are sure to be a hit. You can easily spice things up with the addition of some dried chili or cayenne pepper.

Method:

1. Prepare the carrots by peeling, trimming the ends and slicing them on a mandolin set to ⅛ inch (3 mm).

2. Place the carrot slices into a large mixing bowl along with the remaining ingredients and use your hands to mix them, until the carrots are evenly covered in the oil and seasonings.

3. Arrange the carrot slices on the dehydrator trays. Avoid overcrowding because air needs to circulate around them.

4. Dry at 125°F (52°C) for 6 to 10 hours, rotating the trays a few times during dehydrating, until crisp. Store in an airtight container at room temperature.

Ingredients:

- 8 medium carrots
- ¼ cup (60 ml) tamari
- 2 tbsp (30 ml) coconut oil, melted
- 2 tbsp (5 g) finely chopped fresh parsley

▲ **Yield:** Varies		▲ **Yield:** 4 servings	
⏱ **Prep time:** Variable		⏱ **Prep time:** 15–20 minutes	
≋ **Drying time:** 8–12 hours		≋ **Drying time:** 6–10 hours	

Jalapeños

Ingredients:

- *Enough jalapeños to fill your dehydrator*

Drying your excess jalapeños (or any other chilies) is a fantastic way of preserving them when you have too many to use. Once dried, you can chop or grind them for use in your favorite dishes.

Method:

1. Prepare the jalapeños by removing the stems and cutting them in half lengthways. Remove the seeds and pith, if desired, for less heat.

2. Arrange the halves on the dehydrator trays. Avoid overcrowding because air needs to circulate around them.

3. Dry at 125°F (52°C) for 8 to 12 hours, rotating the trays a few times during dehydrating, until dry and leathery. Store in an airtight container at room temperature.

Barbeque Sweet Potatoes

Ingredients:

- *2 large sweet potatoes*
- *2 tbsp (30 ml) olive oil*
- *1 tbsp (15 ml) honey*
- *2 tsp (5 g) paprika*
- *1 tsp (3 g) onion and garlic powder (see recipe on page 117)*
- *½ tsp (1 g) ground black pepper*
- *½ tsp (1 g) chili powder*
- *½ tsp (1 g) cayenne pepper*
- *½ tsp (2 g) salt*

A vibrant alternative to traditional potato chips.

Method:

1. Wash or peel the sweet potatoes and slice them on a mandolin set to ⅛ inch (3 mm).

2. Place the slices into a large mixing bowl with all the remaining ingredients and mix until the sweet potatoes are evenly covered in the oil and spices.

3. Arrange the slices on the dehydrator trays.

4. Dry at 125°F (52°C) for 6 to 10 hours, rotating the trays a few times during dehydrating, until crisp.

- △ **Yield:** 4–6 servings
- ◔ **Prep time:** 10–25 minutes
- ♨ **Drying time:** 8–12 hours

- △ **Yield:** 2–4 servings
- ◔ **Prep time:** 10–15 minutes
- ♨ **Drying time:** 3–7 hours

Spicy Pumpkin Chips

Ingredients:

- *1 small pumpkin*
- *2 tbsp (30 ml) coconut oil, melted*
- *2 tbsp (30 ml) maple syrup*
- *1 pinch salt*
- *Pumpkin pie spice, to taste*

Any variety of pumpkin will work for these delicious chips. For thin-skinned varieties, there is no need to peel them, just give them a good scrub.

Method:

1. Prepare the pumpkin by quartering, peeling and cutting into ¼-inch (5 mm) slices with a sharp knife.

2. Place the slices into a large mixing bowl along with the coconut oil, maple syrup and salt. Mix with your hands until the pumpkin slices are evenly coated.

3. Arrange the pumpkin slices on the dehydrator trays. Avoid overcrowding because air needs to circulate.

4. Sprinkle the pumpkin slices lightly with pumpkin pie spice, or to taste.

5. Dry at 125°F (52°C) for 8 to 12 hours, rotating the trays a few times, until dry and crisp. Store in an airtight container at room temperature.

Garlic Zucchini Chips

Ingredients:

- *3 large zucchini*
- *2 tbsp (30 ml) olive oil*
- *2–3 tsp (6–9 g) garlic powder*
- *½ tsp (2 g) salt*
- *2 tbsp (5 g) finely chopped fresh parsley*

Zucchini chips make an extremely healthy alternative to regular potato chips, and the flavorings can easily be changed to suit your tastes.

Method:

1. Prepare the zucchini by trimming the ends and slicing them on a mandolin set to ⅛ inch (3 mm).

2. Place the zucchini slices into a large mixing bowl along with the remaining ingredients and use your hands to mix them, until the zucchini are evenly covered in the oil and seasonings.

3. Arrange the zucchini slices on the dehydrator trays. Avoid overcrowding because air needs to circulate around them.

4. Dry at 125°F (52°C) for 3 to 7 hours, rotating the trays a few times during dehydrating, until crisp. Store in an airtight container at room temperature.

- **Yield:** 2–4 servings
- **Prep time:** 15–20 minutes
- **Drying time:** 6–10 hours

Honey Orange Beet Chips

Ingredients:

- 4 medium beets
- 1 large orange
- 3 tbsp (45 ml) honey
- 1 pinch salt

Avoid turning your hands beet red when preparing these by wearing a pair of disposable gloves. Try different varieties of beet for a nice mix of colors.

Method:

1. Prepare the beets by peeling them, trimming the ends and slicing them on a mandolin set to ⅛ inch (3 mm).

2. Zest and juice the orange into a large mixing bowl, add the honey and salt, and mix well. Place the beet slices into the honey and orange mixture and toss gently with your hands until all the beet slices are evenly coated.

3. Arrange the beet slices on the dehydrator trays. Avoid overcrowding because air needs to circulate around them.

4. Dry at 125°F (52°C) for 6 to 10 hours, rotating the trays a few times during dehydrating, until sticky and crisp. Store in an airtight container at room temperature.

48 : Vegetables

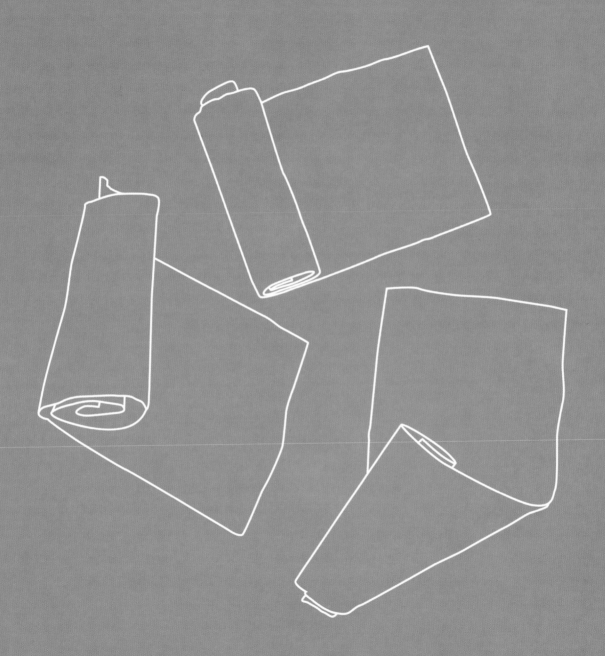

Chapter Four:
Leathers

Kids love fruit leathers, otherwise known as roll-ups. Once you learn how easy it is to make healthier and cheaper roll-ups at home, you'll never look back.

Yield: 12–14 pieces

Prep time: 40–45 minutes

Drying time: 6–10 hours

Ingredients:

- 4 apples
- 1 lb (450 g) strawberries
- 1 lemon, juiced
- 2 tbsp (25 g) granulated sugar (optional)

Strawberry and Apple Leather

Fruit leathers are a great way to use up fruit that's slightly past its best. These make a great snack for kids' lunchboxes; try cutting them into fun shapes for an extra treat.

Method:

1. Prepare the fruit by peeling, coring and dicing the apples into 1-inch (2.5 cm) pieces, and washing and hulling the strawberries.

2. Place the fruit into a medium saucepan with the lemon juice and sugar (if using). Place the saucepan over a medium heat and cook gently, stirring occasionally, until the apples are tender, about 10 to 15 minutes. Remove from the heat and allow the fruit to cool for 15 to 20 minutes.

3. Transfer the fruit to a food processor or blender and process until the mixture is smooth.

4. Spread the fruit puree over dehydrator trays lined with non-stick sheets or baking parchment, approximately ¼ inch (5 mm) thick. Spread the mixture so it's fairly even, but slightly thicker towards the edges, as they will dry first and become brittle otherwise.

5. Dry at 135°F (57°C) for 6 to 10 hours, rotating the trays a few times during dehydrating, until the fruit is dry to the touch and leathery.

6. While the fruit leather is still warm, peel it from the sheets, cut it into 12 to 14 strips, roll them up and allow them to cool before wrapping them in plastic wrap.

7. Store in an airtight container at room temperature.

Blueberry and Lemon Curd Leather

⚠ **Yield:** 12–14 pieces

🕐 **Prep time:** 10–15 minutes

〰 **Drying time:** 8–12 hours

If you are using baking paper to line your dehydrator trays, you needn't peel the leather away once dried; simply cut the paper and leather into strips and roll up as it is.

Ingredients:

- 1 lb (450 g) blueberries, fresh or frozen
- 1 cup (240 ml) applesauce
- ¼ cup (60 ml) lemon curd

Method:

1. Place the blueberries and applesauce into a food processor or blender and process until the mixture is smooth.

2. Spread the fruit puree evenly over dehydrator trays lined with non-stick sheets or baking parchment, approximately ¼ inch (5 mm) thick and 1 inch from the edges. Leave the edges slightly thicker, as they will dry first and become brittle otherwise. Shake the tray lightly from side to side to help even out the mixture.

3. Place the lemon curd into a piping bag and pipe lines of lemon curd across the blueberry puree.

4. Dry at 135°F (57°C) for 8 to 12 hours, rotating the trays a few times during dehydrating, until the fruit is dry to the touch and leathery.

5. While the fruit leather is still warm, peel it from the sheets, cut it into 12 to 14 strips, roll them up and allow them to cool before wrapping them in plastic wrap.

6. Store in an airtight container at room temperature.

Yield: 12–14 pieces

Prep time: 40–45 minutes

Drying time: 6–10 hours

Ingredients:

- 6 medium apples
- 3 medium carrots
- 2 tbsp (30 ml) honey
- 1 tbsp (15 ml) lemon juice

Carrot and Apple Leather

These beautiful, orange-colored fruit leathers taste as lovely as they look. Apples, carrots and honey make a delicious combination that's full of goodness. These are a great way to add some extra veggies into your diet.

Method:

1. Prepare the apples and carrots by peeling, coring and dicing the apples into 1-inch (2.5 cm) pieces, and peeling and cutting the carrots into ½-inch (1 cm) pieces.

2. Place the apples and carrots into a medium saucepan with the honey and lemon juice. Place the saucepan over a medium heat and cook gently, stirring occasionally, until the apples and carrots are tender, about 10 to 15 minutes. Remove from the heat and allow the mixture to cool for 15 to 20 minutes.

3. Transfer the carrots and apples to a food processor or blender and process until the mixture is smooth.

4. Spread the puree over dehydrator trays lined with non-stick sheets or baking parchment, approximately ¼ inch (5 mm) thick. Spread the mixture so it's fairly even, but slightly thicker towards the edges, as they will dry first and become brittle otherwise.

5. Dry at 135°F (57°C) for 6 to 10 hours, rotating the trays a few times during dehydrating, until the fruit is dry to the touch and leathery.

6. While the fruit leather is still warm, peel it from the sheets, cut it into 12 to 14 strips, roll them up and allow them to cool before wrapping them in plastic wrap.

7. Store in an airtight container at room temperature.

Zucchini and Pear Leather

△ **Yield:** 12–14 pieces

🕐 **Prep time:** 35–40 minutes

〰 **Drying time:** 6–10 hours

There's no reason why milder tasting vegetables can't make their way into combinations of your favorite fruit leathers. Zucchini has very little taste and adding it to sweeter recipes is a novel way to eat more veggies. Here, they combine with pears and maple syrup for a lovely treat.

Ingredients:

- 4 large, ripe pears
- 2 medium zucchini
- 2 tbsp (30 ml) maple syrup
- 1 tbsp (15 ml) lemon juice

Method:

1. Prepare the pears and zucchini by peeling, coring and dicing the pears into 1-inch (2.5 cm) pieces and dicing the zucchini into 1-inch (2.5 cm) pieces.

2. Place the pears and zucchini into a medium saucepan with the maple syrup and lemon juice. Place the saucepan over a medium heat and cook gently, stirring occasionally, until the pears and zucchini are tender, about 10 to 15 minutes. Remove from the heat and allow the fruit to cool for 15 to 20 minutes.

3. Transfer the mixture to a food processor or blender and process until the mixture is smooth.

4. Spread the puree over dehydrator trays lined with non-stick sheets or baking parchment, approximately ¼ inch (5 mm) thick. Spread the mixture so it's fairly even, but slightly thicker towards the edges, as they will dry first and become brittle otherwise.

5. Dry at 135°F (57°C) for 6 to 10 hours, rotating the trays a few times during dehydrating, until the fruit is dry to the touch and leathery.

6. While the fruit leather is still warm, peel it from the sheets, cut it into 12 to 14 strips, roll them up and allow them to cool before wrapping them in plastic wrap.

7. Store in an airtight container at room temperature.

Yield: 12–14 pieces

Prep time: 10–15 minutes

Drying time: 6–10 hours

Vanilla Cherry and Banana Leather

Ingredients:

- *3 large, ripe bananas*
- *1 lb (450 g) pitted cherries, fresh or frozen*
- *2 tsp (10 ml) vanilla extract*

Fruit leather is a great way to use up those mushy, over-ripe bananas. In this recipe, the bananas add lovely sweetness to the tart cherries and the vanilla adds an extra depth of flavor, making this fruit leather quite sophisticated.

Method:

1. Prepare the bananas by peeling and cutting into 1-inch (2.5 cm) pieces.

2. Place the banana, cherries and vanilla into a food processor or blender and process until the mixture is smooth.

3. Spread the fruit puree evenly over dehydrator trays lined with non-stick sheets or baking parchment, approximately ¼ inch (5 mm) thick and 1 inch from the edges. Leave the edges slightly thicker, as they will dry first and become brittle otherwise. Shake the tray lightly from side to side to help even out the mixture.

4. Dry at 135°F (57°C) for 6 to 10 hours, rotating the trays a few times during dehydrating, until the fruit is dry to the touch and leathery.

5. While the fruit leather is still warm, peel it from the sheets, cut it into 12 to 14 strips, roll them up and allow them to cool before wrapping them in plastic wrap.

6. Store in an airtight container at room temperature.

Chocolate Cherry Leather

> ▲ **Yield:** 12–14 pieces
>
> ⏱ **Prep time:** 35–40 minutes
>
> ♨ **Drying time:** 6–10 hours

Ingredients:

- 1 lb (450 g) cherries
- 2 tbsp (25 g) granulated sugar
- 2 tbsp (30 ml) water
- 2 tbsp (14 g) cocoa powder

A grown-up twist on the usual fruit leather, this one combines the rich flavors of cherries and chocolate. Because of the cocoa, this leather is more delicate than traditional fruit leathers and best dried on parchment paper, and left on the paper for cutting and storage.

Method:

1. Prepare the cherries by removing the stems and pits using a cherry pitter.

2. Place the cherries, sugar and water into a saucepan and cook over a medium heat for 10 minutes, until the cherries have softened.

3. Stir the cocoa powder into the cherries and cook for 1 minute longer. Remove the mixture from the heat and allow it to cool for 15 to 20 minutes.

4. Transfer the cherry mixture to a food processor or blender and process until the mixture is smooth.

5. Spread the fruit puree evenly over dehydrator trays lined with baking parchment, approximately ¼ inch (5 mm) thick and 1 inch (2.5 cm) from the edges. Leave the edges slightly thicker, as they will dry first and become brittle otherwise. Shake the tray lightly from side to side to help even out the mixture.

6. Dry at 135°F (57°C) for 6 to 10 hours, rotating the trays a few times during dehydrating, until the fruit is dry to the touch and leathery.

7. While the fruit leather is still warm, cut it into 12 to 14 strips, roll them up and allow them to cool before wrapping them in plastic wrap.

8. Store in an airtight container at room temperature.

Almond Cherry Leather

▲ **Yield:** 12–14 pieces

🕐 **Prep time:** 10–15 minutes

♨ **Drying time:** 10–14 hours

The addition of almond butter in these fruit leathers makes a lovely flavor and texture difference. These are best left on the baking parchment they dried on, as the fat from the almonds makes the fruit leather a little less robust.

Ingredients:

- *1 cup (240 ml) applesauce*
- *1 cup (240 ml) cherry jelly*
- *½ cup (120 ml) almond butter*
- *½ cup (40 g) flaked almonds*

Method:

1. Place the applesauce, cherry jelly and almond butter into a food processor or blender and process until the mixture is smooth.

2. Spread the mixture over dehydrator trays lined with baking parchment, approximately ¼ inch (5 mm) thick. Spread the mixture so it's fairly even, but slightly thicker towards the edges, as they will dry first and become brittle otherwise.

3. Sprinkle the flaked almonds evenly over the fruit mixture.

4. Dry at 135°F (57°C) for 10 to 14 hours, rotating the trays a few times during dehydrating, until the fruit is dry to the touch and leathery.

5. While the fruit leather is still warm, cut it into 12 to 14 strips, roll them up and allow them to cool before wrapping them in plastic wrap.

6. Store in an airtight container at room temperature.

Peanut Butter and Jelly Leather

Yield: 12–14 pieces

Prep time: 10–15 minutes

Drying time: 10–14 hours

These are a great take on the classic peanut butter and jelly combination. We've used strawberry jelly here, but feel free to change it for your favorite flavor. These are best left on the baking parchment they dried on, as the fat from the peanut butter makes the fruit leather a little less robust.

Ingredients:

- 1 cup (240 ml) applesauce
- 1 cup (240 ml) strawberry jelly
- ½ cup (120 ml) peanut butter

Method:

1. Place the applesauce, strawberry jelly and peanut butter into a food processor or blender and process until the mixture is smooth.

2. Spread the mixture over dehydrator trays lined with baking parchment, approximately ¼ inch (5 mm) thick. Spread the mixture so it's fairly even, but slightly thicker towards the edges, as they will dry first and become brittle otherwise.

3. Dry at 135°F (57°C) for 10 to 14 hours, rotating the trays a few times during dehydrating, until the fruit is dry to the touch and leathery.

4. While the fruit leather is still warm, cut it into 12 to 14 strips, roll them up and allow them to cool before wrapping them in plastic wrap.

5. Store in an airtight container at room temperature.

- **Yield:** 6–8 pieces
- **Prep time:** 45–50 minutes
- **Drying time:** 6–10 hours

Salted Caramel Apple Leather

Ingredients:

- *4 medium apples*
- *3 tbsp (35 g) granulated sugar*
- *¼ tsp (1 g) salt, to taste*

Salted caramel apple leather is a modern twist on the classic caramel apple flavor, with the addition of a little salt. When preparing the caramel, take great care not to burn yourself, as molten caramel is extremely hot and sticky, and can cause serious burns. It's best to have no distractions when preparing this one.

Method:

1. Prepare the apples by peeling, coring with an apple corer and cutting them into ½-inch (1 cm) pieces with a sharp knife.

2. Prepare the salted caramel by placing a large, heavy-based frying pan over a medium-high heat. Once the pan is hot, sprinkle the granulated sugar evenly over the surface of the pan. Once the sugar has melted, stir it gently with a metal spoon so that it colors evenly. Cook the caramel until it is quite dark, but not burnt; about 5 minutes.

3. Quickly remove the pan from the heat and add the diced apples and salt. Stir the apples through the caramel until the mixture has cooled a little.

4. Return the caramel apples to the heat and cook gently, until the apples have softened; about 10 minutes.

5. Remove from the heat and allow the apples to cool for 20 minutes.

6. Place the caramel apples into a food processor or blender and process until the mixture is smooth.

7. Spread the fruit puree evenly over dehydrator trays lined with non-stick sheets or baking parchment, approximately ¼ inch (5 mm) thick and 1 inch from the edges. Leave the edges slightly thicker, as they will dry first and become brittle otherwise. Shake the tray lightly from side to side to help even out the mixture.

8. Dry at 135°F (57°C) for 6 to 10 hours, rotating the trays a few times during dehydrating, until the fruit is dry to the touch and leathery.

9. While the fruit leather is still warm, peel it from the sheets, cut it into 6 to 8 strips, roll them up and allow them to cool before wrapping them in plastic wrap.

10. Store in an airtight container at room temperature.

> ⚠ **Yield:** 12–14 pieces
> 🕐 **Prep time:** 15–20 minutes
> 💨 **Drying time:** 6–10 hours

Polka Dot Fruit Leather

Ingredients:

- *2 apricots*
- *⅓ cup (35 g) raspberries*
- *⅓ cup (45 g) blueberries*
- *2 cups (480 ml) applesauce*

Add bursts of flavor and contrasting patterns to traditional fruit leather with the addition of polka dots from different fruit combinations. Let your imagination go wild with different flavors. These are a great way to use seasonal fruit.

Method:

1. Prepare the apricots by cutting along their vertical crease. Twist each half in opposite directions to separate them from the pit. Discard the pit.

2. Use a food processor or blender to puree each of the apricots, raspberries and blueberries individually.

3. Spread the applesauce over dehydrator trays lined with non-stick sheets or baking paper, approximately ¼ inch (5 mm) thick. Spread the mixture so it's fairly even, but slightly thicker towards the edges, as they will dry first and become brittle otherwise.

4. Use a small spoon to drop ½ teaspoonful (2 ml) of each of the three different purees onto the applesauce to create the polka dot effect.

5. Dry at 135°F (57°C) for 6 to 10 hours, rotating the trays a few times during dehydrating, until the fruit is dry to the touch and leathery.

6. While the fruit leather is still warm, peel it from the sheets, cut it into 12 to 14 strips, roll them up and allow them to cool before wrapping them in plastic wrap.

7. Store in an airtight container at room temperature.

Chapter Five:
Jerky

The world of jerky is exciting and flavorful. You can dehydrate many different types of meat and fish, so there is always a low-fat, high-protein snack ready to go.

Classic Beef Jerky

Yield: 10–12 servings

Prep time: 12 hours 30 minutes

Drying time: 6–10 hours

Ingredients:

- 2 lb (900 g) lean beef flank
- ½ cup (120 ml) soy sauce
- ½ cup (120 ml) Worcestershire sauce
- 2 tbsp (30 ml) honey
- 1 tbsp (15 ml) liquid smoke
- 2 tsp (4 g) ground black pepper
- 2 tsp (6 g) garlic powder
- Dried chili flakes, to taste

We suggest using flank or any other lean cut of beef for jerky. The reason for using lean meat is that fat can turn rancid and cause the jerky to spoil. You can easily change any of the seasonings in this recipe to suit your tastes.

Method:

1. Prepare the beef by cutting away all visible fat and slicing it with the grain into ¼-inch (5 mm) thick by 1-inch (2.5 cm) wide strips.

2. Prepare the marinade by placing the soy sauce, Worcestershire sauce, honey, liquid smoke, black pepper and garlic powder into a large mixing bowl and mixing well.

3. Add the beef strips to the bowl and mix until all the beef is well coated in the marinade. Press the beef down into the marinade as much as possible, cover the bowl with plastic wrap and refrigerate the beef for 6 to 12 hours, or overnight.

4. Remove the beef strips from the marinade and pull each strip flat and straight before arranging them on the dehydrator trays. Avoid overcrowding because air needs to circulate around them.

5. Sprinkle lightly with chili flakes, or to taste.

6. Dry at 155°F (68°C) for 6 to 10 hours, rotating the trays a few times during dehydrating, until the meat is dry to the touch and cracks, but doesn't break, when bent. Store in an airtight container at room temperature.

Yield: 10–12 servings

Prep time: 2 hours 30 minutes

Drying time: 6–10 hours

Hot and Spicy Beef Jerky

Ingredients:

- *2 lb (900 g) lean beef flank*
- *2 tbsp (30 g) salt*
- *2 tbsp (25 g) brown sugar*
- *1 tbsp (9 g) onion and garlic powder (see recipe on page 117)*
- *1 tbsp (5 g) paprika*
- *2 tsp (5 g) cayenne pepper*
- *2 tsp (4 g) chili flakes*

When slicing meat for jerky, freezing the whole piece of meat for an hour or so will make slicing it into even pieces so much easier. If you have an electric slicer, this is perfect for the job.

Method:

1. Prepare the beef by cutting away all visible fat and slicing it with the grain into ¼-inch (5 mm) thick by 1-inch (2.5 cm) wide strips.

2. Prepare the dry rub by placing all the dry ingredients into a large mixing bowl and mixing well.

3. Add the beef strips to the rub and toss until all the beef is well coated in the spices. Cover the bowl with plastic wrap and refrigerate the beef for 1 to 2 hours.

4. Remove the beef strips from the bowl, dust off any excess rub and pull each strip flat and straight before arranging them on the dehydrator trays. Avoid overcrowding because air needs to circulate around them.

5. Dry at 155°F (68°C) for 6 to 10 hours, rotating the trays a few times during dehydrating, until the meat is dry to the touch and cracks, but doesn't break, when bent. Store in an airtight container at room temperature.

Teriyaki Beef Jerky

> ⚠ **Yield:** 10–12 servings
>
> ⏱ **Prep time:** 12 hours 30 minutes
>
> ♨ **Drying time:** 6–10 hours

How you slice your meat changes the finished jerky; meat sliced with the grain produces a chewy jerky, but meat sliced across the grain will be more tender.

Method:

1. Prepare the beef as per the Hot and Spicy recipe on page 72.

2. Place the other ingredients into a large mixing bowl and mix well to make the marinade.

3. Add the beef to the marinade and mix until it is well coated. Cover the bowl with plastic wrap and refrigerate for 6 to 12 hours, or overnight.

4. Remove the beef from the marinade and pull each strip flat before arranging on the dehydrator trays.

5. Dry at 155°F (68°C) for 6 to 10 hours, until the meat is dry to the touch and cracks, but doesn't break, when bent.

Ingredients:

- 2 lb (900 g) lean beef flank
- ⅔ cup (160 ml) soy sauce
- ⅓ cup (80 ml) mirin (rice wine)
- 3 tbsp (40 g) brown sugar
- 1 tbsp (9 g) onion and garlic powder (see recipe on page 117)
- 2 tsp (10 g) fresh, grated ginger

Chinese Pork Jerky

This recipe uses pork mince; get the lowest fat, freshest mince you can find or, preferably, mince the pork yourself. Once dried, the pork is placed into a very hot oven to char the edges slightly and increase the flavor. You could also char it lightly on a hot grill.

Method:

1. Place all of the ingredients into a large mixing bowl and mix well, massaging the spices into the pork, until the meat becomes quite gooey.

2. Cover the bowl with plastic wrap and refrigerate the pork for 6 to 12 hours, or overnight.

3. Use a rolling pin to roll the pork mince between baking parchment until it is ¼ inch (5 mm) thick.

4. Remove the top sheet of baking parchment and place the sheets of pork onto the dehydrator trays.

5. Dry at 155°F (68°C) for 6 to 12 hours, rotating the trays a few times during dehydrating. Peel the dried pork from the baking parchment once it is dry enough to hold together and flip it over for the remaining drying time.

6. Pre-heat the oven to 425°F (220°C).

7. Cut the pork into 3-inch (7.5 cm) squares.

8. Transfer the dried pork squares to baking trays and bake in the oven until the edges of the pork have charred slightly, about 5 to 10 minutes. Remove the pork from the oven and place on a wire rack to cool.

9. Store in an airtight container at room temperature.

Ingredients:

- *2 lb (900 g) lean pork mince (less than 10% fat)*
- *1 tbsp (15 ml) fish sauce*
- *2 tbsp (30 ml) light soy sauce*
- *2 tbsp (30 ml) dark soy sauce*
- *1 tbsp (15 ml) sesame oil*
- *2 tbsp (30 ml) mirin (rice wine)*
- *½ cup (110 g) granulated sugar*
- *1 tsp (2 g) ground black pepper*
- *2 tsp (3 g) Chinese five spice*
- *1 tsp (2 g) ground cinnamon*
- *½ tsp (1 g) ground star anise*

Salmon Jerky

Ingredients:

- *1 skinless side of salmon, bones removed*
- *1 cup (240 ml) tamari*
- *2 tbsp (35 g) brown sugar*
- *2 tbsp (30 ml) lemon juice*
- *2 tsp (4 g) ground black pepper*

As salmon is an oily fish, it's best to store the finished jerky in the refrigerator or freezer, as the oil can turn rancid and spoil the jerky. As with all fish jerky, use only the freshest fish.

Method:

1. Prepare the salmon by cutting it crossways into 4-inch (10 cm) pieces then slice these lengthways into ¼-inch (5 mm) strips. As the salmon is not a uniform thickness from its head to its tail, you will probably end up with some strips that are much thicker than others, cut these in half so all are a similar size.

2. Prepare the marinade by placing the tamari, brown sugar, lemon juice and black pepper into a large mixing bowl and mixing well.

3. Add the salmon strips to the marinade and mix until all the salmon is well coated in the marinade. Press the salmon down into the marinade as much as possible, cover the bowl with plastic wrap and refrigerate the salmon for 1 to 3 hours.

4. Remove the salmon strips from the marinade and pat them dry on paper towel before arranging them on the dehydrator trays. Avoid overcrowding because air needs to circulate around them.

5. Dry at 155°F (68°C) for 10 to 16 hours, rotating the trays a few times during dehydrating, until the jerky is dry, but still flexible. Store in an airtight container in the refrigerator.

Dried Shrimp

⚠ **Yield:** Varies

🕐 **Prep time:** Variable

〰 **Drying time:** 6–12 hours

These tasty dried shrimp are great for adding to dehydrated meals while camping, using in Asian or Cajun style dishes, as a crunchy little addition to salads or as a snack in their own right. There's no need to shell the shrimp if they are tiny, you may prefer to if they are larger.

Method:

1. Arrange the shrimp on the dehydrator trays. Avoid overcrowding because air needs to circulate around them.

2. Dry at 125°F (52°C) for 6 to 12 hours, rotating the trays a few times during dehydrating, until dry and crisp. Store in an airtight container at room temperature.

Ingredients:

- *Enough cooked shrimp to fill your dehydrator*

> **Yield:** About 24 pieces
>
> **Prep time:** 7 hours
>
> **Drying time:** 6–12 hours

Salt Cod Jerky

Ingredients:

- *2 lb (900 g) fresh, skinless cod fillets*
- *6 cups (1.44 l) water*
- *2 ¾ cups (660 g) salt*
- *2 tbsp (6 g) dried mixed herbs*
- *2 tsp (6 g) lemon zest*
- *1 tbsp (9 g) garlic powder*

Salt cod jerky is a classic way of preserving fish. Use only the freshest fish to lower the risk of spoilage during the drying process. The finished jerky should have only a mild fishy taste and aroma. Use as you would any salted fish.

Method:

1. Prepare the cod by slicing it into ¼-inch (2 mm) thick by 1-inch (2.5 cm) wide strips.

2. Mix the ¾ cup (180 g) of the salt with 6 cups (1.44 l) of water to make a brine.

3. Place the cod into the brine for 30 minutes.

4. Remove the fish from the brine and rinse away the salt under cold, running water. Pat the fish dry using paper towel.

5. Prepare the dry cure by mixing the remaining 2 cups (480 g) of salt with the dried herbs, lemon zest and garlic powder.

6. Place the fish into the dry cure, making sure each piece is covered in salt. Store in an airtight container in the fridge for 6 hours.

7. Remove the fish strips from the dry cure, dusting off any excess salt, and pull each strip flat and straight before arranging them on the dehydrator trays. Avoid overcrowding because air needs to circulate around them.

8. Dry at 155°F (68°C) for 6 to 12 hours, rotating the trays a few times during dehydrating, until the fish is dry and has no visible surface moisture. Store in an airtight container at room temperature.

Chapter Six:
Nuts and Seeds

Nuts and seeds make the perfect snack — high in protein, full of healthy fats and yummy, too! This chapter gives you some fun recipes that will soon become your pantry staples.

⚠ Yield: 4 cups (570 g)

🕐 Prep time: 10–15 minutes

〰 Drying time: 18–24 hours

Spicy Nut and Seed Mix

Ingredients:

- *1 cup (150 g) raw almonds, soaked and drained*
- *1 cup (140 g) raw cashews, soaked and drained*
- *1 cup (135 g) raw macadamias*
- *1 cup (135 g) raw pepitas, soaked and drained*
- *2 tsp (4 g) chili powder*
- *1 tsp (2 g) ground black pepper*
- *1 tbsp (5 g) paprika*
- *1 tbsp (3 g) garlic powder*
- *1 tbsp (3 g) dried oregano*
- *3 tsp (15 g) salt*
- *Cayenne pepper, to taste*

Feel free to change the nuts and seeds in this recipe for what you have readily available, these flavors lend themselves to any combination.

Method:

1. Place the nuts and pepitas into a large mixing bowl and add the remaining ingredients, except the cayenne pepper. Mix well, until all the nuts and seeds are well coated.

2. Arrange the nuts and seeds on the dehydrator trays and sprinkle lightly, or to taste, with cayenne pepper. Avoid overcrowding because air needs to circulate around them.

3. Dry at 125°F (52°C) for 18 to 24 hours, rotating the trays a few times during dehydrating, until the nuts are dry and crisp. Store in an airtight container at room temperature.

Yield: 4 cups (450 g)

Prep time: 10–15 minutes

Drying time: 16–18 hours

Cajun Pecans

Ingredients:

- *4 cups (440 g) raw pecans, soaked and drained*
- *2 tsp (3 g) ground coriander*
- *2 tsp (3 g) ground cumin*
- *2 tsp (5 g) paprika*
- *1 tsp (3 g) onion and garlic powder (see recipe on page 117)*
- *1 tbsp (3 g) dried oregano*
- *2 tsp (10 g) salt*
- *¼ tsp (½ g) ground black pepper*

Like all nuts, pecans lend themselves perfectly to both sweet and savory dishes. In this recipe they are the ideal carrier for this blend of Cajun spices. Because of their high oil content, the finished nuts should be stored in the refrigerator if being kept for longer periods of time, to prevent them becoming rancid.

Method:

1. Place the pecans and remaining ingredients into a large mixing bowl and toss well until all the pecans are coated in the spice mixture.

2. Arrange the pecans on the dehydrator trays. Avoid overcrowding because air needs to circulate around them.

3. Dry at 125°F (52°C) for 16 to 18 hours, rotating the trays a few times during dehydrating, until the nuts are dry and crisp. Store in an airtight container in the refrigerator.

Spiced Pepitas

Yield: 4 cups (560 g)

Prep time: 10–15 minutes

Drying time: 8–12 hours

Spiced pepitas (pumpkins seeds) make a delicious, moreish snack on their own or a flavorful addition to trail mix or salads. They can even be added to desserts for extra texture and flavor.

Method:

1. Place the coconut oil and honey into a large mixing bowl and mix well.

2. Add the remaining ingredients and toss well until all the pepitas are coated in the spice mixture.

3. Arrange the pepitas on the dehydrator trays. Avoid overcrowding because air needs to circulate around them.

4. Dry at 125°F (52°C) for 8 to 12 hours, rotating the trays a few times during dehydrating, until the seeds are dry and crisp. Store in an airtight container at room temperature.

Ingredients:

- 2 tbsp (30 ml) coconut oil, melted
- 3 tbsp (45 ml) honey
- 4 cups (540 g) raw pepitas, soaked and drained
- 1 tsp (2 g) ground cinnamon
- ½ tsp (1 g) ground ginger
- ½ tsp (1 g) ground star anise
- ½ tsp (1 g) allspice

Yield: 4 cups (580 g)

Prep time: 10–15 minutes

Drying time: 12–16 hours

Chipotle Lime Cashews

Ingredients:

- *2 fresh limes*
- *2 tsp (5 g) ground chipotle, to taste*
- *2 tbsp (25 g) brown sugar*
- *2 tsp (10 g) salt*
- *4 cups (560 g) raw cashews, soaked and drained*

These chipotle lime cashews are the perfect blend of sweet, sour and spicy. A great snack for your next party — or anytime, really. You can add more or less chipotle, depending on your preference.

Method:

1. Zest and juice the limes into a large mixing bowl.

2. Add the ground chipotle, brown sugar and salt to the lime juice and zest, and mix well.

3. Place the cashews into the chipotle lime mixture and lightly toss until all the cashews are evenly coated.

4. Arrange the cashews on the dehydrator trays. Avoid overcrowding because air needs to circulate around them.

5. Dry at 125°F (52°C) for 12 to 16 hours, rotating the trays a few times during dehydrating, until the nuts are dry and crisp. Store in an airtight container at room temperature.

Salted Honey Walnuts

⚠ **Yield:** 4 cups (420 g)

🕐 **Prep time:** 2 hours 10 minutes

〰 **Drying time:** 18–24 hours

The addition of salt to these honeyed walnuts adds a real flavor punch — these nuts are seriously addictive! Try using different types of honey for subtle flavor variations. The honey will take quite some time to dry, and still be quite sticky once done.

Method:

1. Place the walnuts into a large mixing bowl, add the honey and salt, and mix well.

2. Allow the walnuts to marinate in the honey for 2 hours, stirring occasionally.

3. Arrange the walnuts on dehydrator trays lined with non-stick sheets or baking parchment and drizzle any remaining honey over the top. Avoid overcrowding because air needs to circulate around them.

4. Dry at 125°F (52°C) for 18 to 24 hours, rotating the trays a few times during dehydrating, until the nuts are crisp and sticky. Store in an airtight container at room temperature.

Ingredients:

- *4 cups (400 g) raw walnuts, soaked and drained*
- *¼ cup (60 ml) honey*
- *2 tsp (10 g) salt*

Pine Nuts with Thyme and Sesame

Ingredients:

- 1 cup (140 g) raw pine nuts
- 1 tbsp (3 g) fresh thyme leaves
- 1 tbsp (10 g) sesame seeds
- 2 tsp (10 ml) olive oil
- ½ tsp (2 g) salt

Pine nuts make a wonderful addition to so many dishes, and the thyme and sesame in this recipe just adds to their flavor. Try them in salads or sprinkled over your favorite savory meal for extra crunch.

Method:

1. Place the pine nuts, thyme, sesame seeds, olive oil and salt into a medium mixing bowl and toss well until all the pine nuts are coated in the thyme and sesame seeds.

2. Arrange the pine nuts on the dehydrator trays. Avoid overcrowding because air needs to circulate around them.

3. Dry at 125°F (52°C) for 4 to 8 hours, rotating the trays a few times during dehydrating, until the nuts are dry and crisp. Store in an airtight container at room temperature.

Chocolate Vanilla Hazelnuts

Chocolate and hazelnuts is a match made in heaven, and the addition of vanilla brings an extra depth of flavor.

Method:

1. Combine the coconut oil, cocoa powder, brown sugar and vanilla extract in a large mixing bowl and mix well.

2. Place the hazelnuts into the chocolate mixture and lightly toss until all the hazelnuts are evenly coated.

3. Arrange the hazelnuts on the dehydrator trays. Avoid overcrowding because air needs to circulate around them.

4. Dry at 125°F (52°C) for 18 to 24 hours, rotating the trays a few times during dehydrating, until the nuts are dry and crisp. Store in an airtight container at room temperature.

Ingredients:

- *3 tbsp (45 ml) coconut oil, melted*
- *3 tbsp (20 g) cocoa powder*
- *¼ cup (50 g) brown sugar*
- *2 tsp (10 ml) vanilla extract*
- *4 cups (560 g) raw hazelnuts, soaked and drained*

Cinnamon Chocolate Almonds

Ingredients:

- 3 tbsp (45 ml) coconut oil, melted
- 3 tbsp (20 g) cocoa powder
- ¼ cup (50 g) brown sugar
- 2 tsp (5 g) ground cinnamon
- 4 cups (600 g) raw almonds, soaked and drained

Chocolate and almonds go together wonderfully, and cinnamon adds a subtle hint of spice and warmth. These nuts are best stored in the refrigerator, due to the oil content.

Method:

1. Combine the coconut oil, cocoa powder, brown sugar and ground cinnamon in a large mixing bowl and mix well.

2. Place the almonds into the chocolate mixture and lightly toss until all the almonds are evenly coated.

3. Arrange the almonds on the dehydrator trays.
Avoid overcrowding because air needs to circulate around them.

4. Dry at 125°F (52°C) for 18 to 24 hours, rotating the trays a few times during dehydrating, until the nuts are dry and crisp. Store in an airtight container in the refrigerator.

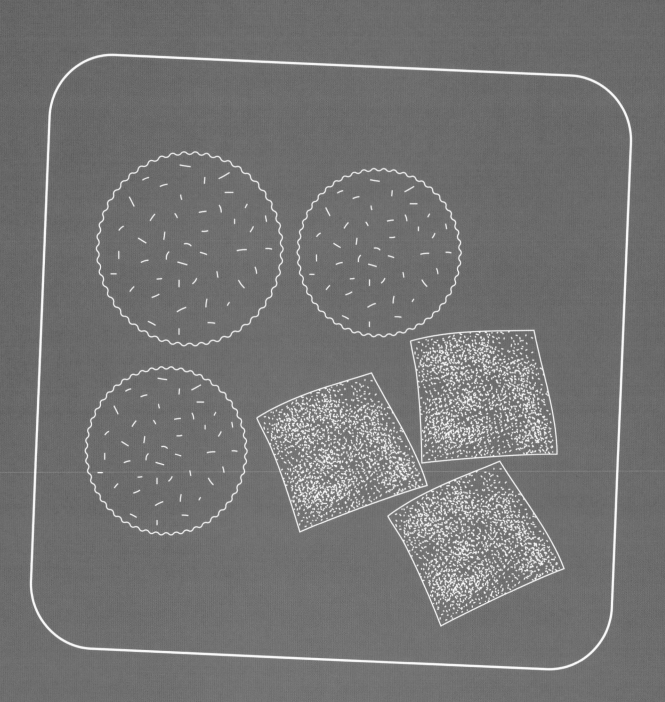

Chapter Seven:
Crackers and Flatbreads

Possibly the most delicious and inventive of all dehydrated creations, crackers and flatbreads are great raw, gluten-free alternatives to traditional sandwich breads and wraps.

Yield: 24 crispbreads

Prep time: 2 hours 15 minutes

Drying time: 14–23 hours

Buckwheat Crispbreads

Ingredients:

- *3 cups (510 g) raw buckwheat groats, soaked and drained*
- *1 cup (130 g) raw sunflower seeds, soaked and drained*
- *1 cup (90 g) ground flaxseed*
- *1 tbsp (9 g) garlic powder*
- *2 tbsp (6 g) fresh thyme leaves*
- *1 tsp (5 g) salt*

Buckwheat groats are crunchy whole buckwheat seeds; they are a wonderful grain-free alternative to wheat, oats and barley. These crispbreads are completely free of grains and gluten, perfect for a light lunch.

Method:

1. Place the buckwheat groats and sunflower seeds into the bowl of a food processor and add the remaining ingredients. Process the mixture until it forms a well-combined, sticky dough.

2. Use a spatula to evenly spread the buckwheat mixture onto dehydrator trays lined with non-stick sheets or baking parchment until it is around ¼ inch (5 mm) thick.

3. Use the back of a knife to score the sheets of buckwheat into 2-inch (5 cm) by 4-inch (10 cm) rectangles.

4. Dry at 155°F (68°C) for the first 2 to 3 hours of drying, then reduce the temperature to 115°F (46°C) for 12 to 20 hours, flipping the crispbreads over after 6 hours and peeling away the non-stick sheet.

5. Rotate the trays a few times during dehydrating, until the crispbreads are dry and crisp. Store in an airtight container at room temperature.

Corn Chips

▲ **Yield:** 45–50 chips

🕐 **Prep time:** 15–20 minutes

〰️ **Drying time:** 14–23 hours

Ingredients:

- 4 cups (600 g) fresh corn kernels
- 1 cup (90 g) ground flaxseed
- 1 medium brown onion, chopped
- 2 tsp (3 g) paprika
- 2 tsp (3 g) ground cumin
- 1 tsp (5 g) salt

It's so easy to make your own delicious corn chips, free of oil and additives and completely raw. Use either fresh or frozen corn; the end result will be the same: crispy, tasty corn chips.

Method:

1. To prepare the corn chips, place all the ingredients into the bowl of a food processor and process until the mixture is well combined and fairly smooth.

2. Use a spatula to evenly spread the corn mixture onto dehydrator trays lined with non-stick sheets or baking parchment until it is around ⅛ inch (3 mm) thick.

3. Use the back of a knife to score the sheets of corn into 2-inch (5 cm) triangles.

4. Dry at 155°F (68°C) for the first 2 to 3 hours of drying, then reduce the temperature to 115°F (46°C) for 12 to 20 hours, flipping the corn chips over after 6 hours and peeling away the non-stick sheet.

5. Rotate the trays a few times during dehydrating, until the corn chips are dry and crisp. Store in an airtight container at room temperature.

Onion and Poppy Seed Crackers

Ingredients:

- 3 cups (300 g) finely chopped white onion
- ½ cup (75 g) ground chia seeds
- 1 cup (100 g) almond meal
- ½ cup (70 g) poppy seeds
- ½ tsp (2 g) salt

Onion and poppy seeds make these crackers not only tasty, but also lovely to look at. These raw crackers would lend themselves well to any savory topping. For best results, use a food processor to chop the onion.

Method:

1. To prepare the crackers, place all the ingredients into a large mixing bowl and stir until the mixture is well combined. Let the mixture sit for 15 to 20 minutes to allow the ground chia to gel.

2. Use a spatula to evenly spread the onion mixture onto dehydrator trays lined with non-stick sheets or baking parchment until it is around ¼ inch (5 mm) thick.

3. Use the back of a knife to score the sheets of onion mixture into 2-inch (5 cm) squares.

4. Dry at 155°F (68°C) for the first 2 to 3 hours of drying, then reduce the temperature to 115°F (46°C) for 12 to 20 hours, flipping the crackers over after 6 hours and peeling away the non-stick sheet.

5. Rotate the trays a few times during dehydrating, until the crackers are dry and crisp. Store in an airtight container at room temperature.

Flaxseed Crackers

▲ **Yield:** 36 crackers

🕐 **Prep time:** 2 hours 15 minutes

〰 **Drying time:** 14–23 hours

This basic cracker recipe lends itself to a range of flavors. Try different variations using your favorite herbs, or vegetables such as dried tomatoes, dried radishes or garlic and onion powder.

Method:

1. To prepare the flaxseed, place it into a large mixing bowl with the 2 cups (480 ml) of water and mix well. Allow the flaxseed to soak for 1 to 2 hours, until the mixture is thick and gelatinous.

2. Add the Italian herb seasoning and salt to the flaxseeds and mix well.

3. Use a spatula to evenly spread the flaxseed mixture onto dehydrator trays lined with non-stick sheets or baking parchment until it is around ¼ inch (5 mm) thick.

4. Use the back of a knife to score the sheets of flaxseed into 2-inch (5 cm) squares.

5. Dry at 155°F (68°C) for the first 2 to 3 hours of drying, then reduce the temperature to 115°F (46°C) for 12 to 20 hours, flipping the crackers over after 6 hours and rotating the trays a few times during dehydrating, until the crackers are dry and crisp. Store in an airtight container at room temperature.

Ingredients:

- *2 cups (260 g) brown flaxseed*
- *2 cups (480 ml) water*
- *2 tbsp (6 g) Italian herb seasoning*
- *1 tsp (5 g) salt*

Walnut and Cranberry Crackers

⚠ **Yield:** 24 crackers

🕐 **Prep time:** 15–20 minutes

〰 **Drying time:** 14–23 hours

These walnut and cranberry crackers would make a lovely addition to a cheese platter or snack plate, or a delicious treat on their own.

Ingredients:

- *3 cups (300 g) raw walnuts, soaked and drained*
- *½ cup (45 g) ground flaxseed*
- *¼ cup (60 ml) water*
- *½ cup (80 g) dried cranberries*
- *½ tsp (2 g) salt*

Method:

1. Place the walnuts, ground flaxseed and water into the bowl of a food processor and process until well combined and fairly smooth.

2. Add the cranberries and salt to the food processor and pulse a few times to combine and roughly chop the cranberries into the walnut mixture.

3. Use a spatula to evenly spread the walnut mixture onto dehydrator trays lined with non-stick sheets or baking parchment until it is around ¼ inch (5 mm) thick.

4. Use the back of a knife to score the sheets of walnut mixture into 2-inch (5 cm) squares.

5. Dry at 155°F (68°C) for the first 2 to 3 hours of drying, then reduce the temperature to 115°F (46°C) for 12 to 20 hours, flipping the crackers over after 6 hours and peeling away the non-stick sheet.

6. Rotate the trays a few times during dehydrating, until the crackers are dry and crisp. Store in an airtight container at room temperature.

Sunflower Seed Bread

Ingredients:

- 1 cup (130 g) golden flaxseed
- 1 cup (240 ml) water
- 3 cups (390 g) sunflower seeds, soaked and drained
- ½ cup (45 g) ground flaxseed
- ½ cup (35 g) psyllium husk
- ½ cup (100 g) sundried tomato
- 1 tbsp (3 g) garlic powder
- 1 tsp (5 g) salt

This bread is shaped into a loaf, then sliced partway through drying. If you can't get to the dehydrator during the drying process, you can shape the dough into ½-inch (1 cm) thick discs before drying.

Method:

1. Place the whole golden flaxseed into a large mixing bowl with 1 cup (240 ml) of water and mix well. Leave to soak for 15 to 30 minutes, until the mixture has gelled.

2. Place 2 cups of the sunflower seeds into the bowl of a food processor, reserving the remaining cup for later. Add the whole flaxseed, ground flaxseed and psyllium husk to the food processor and process until the mixture forms a firm dough, adding a little water if necessary.

3. Add the remaining sunflower seeds, sundried tomato, garlic powder and salt to the food processor and pulse a few times to combine and roughly chop the sunflower seeds and sundried tomatoes.

4. Shape the mixture into a rectangular loaf approximately 8 inches (20 cm) by 5 inches (12.5 cm), and place it on a dehydrator tray.

5. Dry at 155°F (68°C) for the first 2 to 3 hours of drying, then reduce the temperature to 115°F (46°C) for 8 hours.

6. Remove the loaf from the dehydrator and slice it into ½-inch (1 cm) slices.

7. Arrange the slices on the dehydrator trays; avoid overcrowding because air needs to circulate around them.

8. Continue drying at 115°F (46°C) for a further 6 to 10 hours, rotating the trays a few times, until the slices of bread are dry, but not crisp. Store in an airtight container in the refrigerator.

Nut-free Flatbread

⚠ **Yield:** 4–6 pieces

🕐 **Prep time:** 15 minutes

♨ **Drying time:** 9–14 hours

This flatbread is completely nut-free, making it a great addition to a school lunchbox, or for people with nut allergies.

Method:

1. Prepare the carrots by peeling, removing the ends and cutting them into 1-inch (2.5 cm) pieces. Remove the ends from the zucchini and cut them into 1-inch (2.5 cm) pieces.

2. Place the carrot, zucchini, pepitas, sunflower seeds, flaxseed and salt into the bowl of a food processor and process until the mixture is finely chopped, but not completely smooth.

3. Use a spatula to evenly spread the flatbread mixture onto dehydrator trays lined with non-stick sheets or baking parchment until it is around ¼ inch (5 mm) thick.

4. Dry at 155°F (68°C) for the first 2 to 3 hours of drying, then reduce the temperature to 115°F (46°C) for 7 to 11 hours, flipping the flatbread over after 6 hours and peeling away the non-stick sheet.

5. Rotate the trays a few times during dehydrating, until the flatbread is dry to the touch and leathery.

6. Cut the flatbread to the desired size and store in an airtight container in the refrigerator.

Ingredients:

- *2 medium carrots*
- *1 medium zucchini*
- *1 cup (135 g) raw pepitas, soaked and drained*
- *1 cup (130 g) raw sunflower seeds, soaked and drained*
- *1 cup (130 g) brown flaxseed*
- *1 tsp (5 g) salt*

Tomato Flatbread

Yield: 4–6 pieces

Prep time: 15–20 minutes

Drying time: 10–15 hours

This flatbread is a fantastic way to use up some overripe tomatoes. Add your favorite fresh herbs to the mixture for extra flavor.

Ingredients:

- *2 cups (280 g) raw cashews, soaked and drained*
- *1 cup (200 g) sundried tomato*
- *3 medium tomatoes, chopped*
- *1 cup (90 g) ground flaxseed*
- *2 tbsp (6 g) dried oregano*
- *½ tsp (2 g) salt*

Method:

1. Place all the ingredients in a food processor and process until the mixture is finely chopped, but not completely smooth.

2. Use a spatula to evenly spread the tomato mixture onto dehydrator trays lined with non-stick sheets or baking parchment until it is around ¼ inch (5 mm) thick.

3. Dry at 155°F (68°C) for the first 2 to 3 hours, then reduce the temperature to 115°F (46°C) for 8 to 12 hours, flipping the flatbread over after 6 hours and peeling away the non-stick sheet.

4. Rotate the trays a few times during dehydrating, until the flatbread is dry to the touch and leathery.

5. Cut the flatbread to the desired size and store in an airtight container in the refrigerator.

Zucchini Flatbread

▲ **Yield:** 4–6 pieces

🕐 **Prep time:** 20–30 minutes

〰 **Drying time:** 10–15 hours

This flatbread is a fantastic way to use up a glut of seasonal zucchini. Packed full of the goodness of green vegetables, it makes a tasty addition to any meal. As with other flatbread recipes, the key is to dry it until it is dry, but still flexible — not completely crisp.

Method:

1. Prepare the zucchini by removing the ends and cutting them into 1-inch (2.5 cm) pieces.

2. Place the zucchini, pepitas, baby spinach, ground chia and salt into the bowl of a food processor and process until the mixture is finely chopped, but not completely smooth.

3. Use a spatula to evenly spread the zucchini mixture onto dehydrator trays lined with non-stick sheets or baking parchment until it is around ¼ inch (5 mm) thick.

4. Dry at 155°F (68°C) for the first 2 to 3 hours of drying, then reduce the temperature to 115°F (46°C) for 8 to 12 hours, flipping the flatbread over after 6 hours and peeling away the non-stick sheet

5. Rotate the trays a few times during dehydrating, until the flatbread is dry to the touch and leathery.

6. Cut the flatbread to the desired size and store in an airtight container in the refrigerator.

Ingredients:

- *3 medium zucchini*
- *1 cup (135 g) raw pepitas, soaked and drained*
- *3 cups (90 g) baby spinach leaves, roughly chopped*
- *½ cup (70 g) ground chia seed*
- *½ tsp (2 g) salt*

Cinnamon Raisin Toast

⚠ **Yield:** 8–10 pieces

🕐 **Prep time:** 2 hours 15 minutes

〰 **Drying time:** 14–19 hours

Who doesn't love the delicious spiced flavors and bursts of sweetness from the raisins of cinnamon raisin toast? This toast is delicious on its own, or served with fresh fruit or nut butter.

Method:

1. Prepare the apples by peeling, coring and dicing them into 1-inch (2.5 cm) pieces.

2. Peel the banana and slice it into 1-inch (2.5 cm) pieces.

3. Place the apple, banana, walnuts, almond meal, ground flaxseed and cinnamon into the bowl of a food processor and process until the mixture is finely chopped, but not completely smooth.

4. Transfer the mixture to a large mixing bowl and stir in the raisins.

5. Use a spatula to evenly spread the raisin toast mixture onto dehydrator trays lined with non-stick sheets or baking parchment until it is around ½ inch (1 cm) thick.

6. Dry at 155°F (68°C) for the first 2 to 3 hours of drying, then reduce the temperature to 115°F (46°C) for 6 hours.

7. Remove the raisin toast from the dehydrator, flip it over, remove the non-stick sheet and slice it into 2-inch (5 cm) by 4-inch (10 cm) rectangles.

8. Arrange the rectangles on the dehydrator trays; avoid overcrowding because air needs to circulate around them.

9. Continue drying at 115°F (46°C) for a further 6 to 10 hours, rotating the trays a few times during dehydrating, until the raisin toast is crisp and dry on the outside, but still a little soft on the inside. Store in an airtight container in the refrigerator.

Ingredients:

- 2 medium apples
- 1 medium banana
- 2 cups (200 g) raw walnuts, soaked and drained
- 1 cup (100 g) almond meal
- 1 cup (90 g) ground flaxseed
- 2 tsp (5 g) ground cinnamon
- ½ cup (100 g) raisins

Chocolate Peanut Butter Chia Seed Squares

Ingredients:

- 2 cups (280 g) raw peanuts, soaked and drained
- I cup (155 g) chia seeds
- I cup (240 ml) water
- 4 fresh dates, stones removed
- 2 tbsp (10 g) raw cacao powder
- ½ tsp (2 g) salt

Chocolate and peanut butter combined with the goodness of chia seeds make these squares not only delicious, but also good for you!

Method:

1. Place the chia seeds into a large mixing bowl with the I cup (240 ml) of water and mix well. Leave the chia to soak for I5 to 30 minutes, until the mixture has gelled.

2. Place the chia seeds, peanuts, dates, raw cacao powder and salt into the bowl of a food processor and process until the mixture is finely chopped, but not completely smooth.

3. Use a spatula to evenly spread the mixture onto dehydrator trays lined with non-stick sheets or baking parchment until it is around ¼ inch (5 mm) thick.

4. Use the back of a knife to score the sheets into 2-inch (5 cm) squares.

5. Dry at 155°F (68°C) for the first 2 to 3 hours of drying, then reduce the temperature to 115°F (46°C) for 12 to 20 hours, flipping the squares over after 6 hours and peeling away the non-stick sheet.

6. Rotate the trays a few times during dehydrating, until the squares are dry and crisp.

7. Store in an airtight container in the refrigerator.

Chapter Eight:

Herbs and Seasonings

Want a way to make all your dishes more interesting, flavorful and spicy? Dehydrating your own fresh herbs and spices to make delicious, long-lasting ingredients and seasonings creates aromatic additions to every meal.

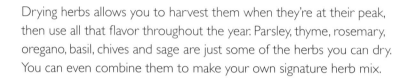

Herbs

Yield: Varies

Prep time: Variable

Drying time: 2–4 hours

Ingredients:

- *Enough fresh herbs to fill your dehydrator*

Drying herbs allows you to harvest them when they're at their peak, then use all that flavor throughout the year. Parsley, thyme, rosemary, oregano, basil, chives and sage are just some of the herbs you can dry. You can even combine them to make your own signature herb mix.

Method:

1. Prepare the herbs by washing them well and patting dry with paper towel.

2. Cut the herbs into small sprigs; don't chop them finely or they'll blow away in the dehydrator. You can remove the leaves from the stems once dry.

3. Arrange the herbs on the dehydrator trays. Avoid overcrowding because air needs to circulate around them.

4. Dry at 115°F (46°C) for 2 to 4 hours, rotating the trays a few times during dehydrating. Store in an airtight container at room temperature.

Onion and Garlic Powder

▲ **Yield:** ½ cup (85 g)

🕐 **Prep time:** 15–20 minutes

♨ **Drying time:** 8–12 hours

Making your own onion and garlic powder will not only save you money, it will also mean you always have this flavorful, versatile ingredient on hand. It makes a great addition to hot dishes, as well as dips and salad dressings.

Ingredients:

- *4 large brown onions*
- *1 bulb garlic*

Method:

1. Prepare the onions by slicing off the ends, cutting them in half and peeling each half.

2. Prepare the garlic by separating and peeling the cloves.

3. Cut the onions and garlic into ¼-inch (5 mm) slices.

4. Arrange the onions and garlic on the dehydrator trays. Avoid overcrowding because air needs to circulate around them.

5. Dry at 115°F (46°C) for 8 to 12 hours, rotating the trays a few times during dehydrating.

6. Once the onions and garlic are completely dry and crisp, place them into a blender or coffee grinder and grind them to a fine powder. Store in an airtight container at room temperature.

- ▲ **Yield:** Varies
- ◷ **Prep time:** Variable
- ♨ **Drying time:** 4–6 hours

- ▲ **Yield:** Varies
- ◷ **Prep time:** Variable
- ♨ **Drying time:** 4–8 hours

Lemon Zest

Ingredients:

- *Enough lemons to fill your dehydrator*

After zesting the lemons for this recipe, slice the fruit into ¼-inch (5 mm) slices and dehydrate them along with the zest. These lemon slices make a lovely addition to fish and other savory dishes, or just for popping into your cup of tea.

Method:

1. Prepare the lemons by using a zester or peeler to remove all of the yellow zest from the lemons, leaving the white pith behind.

2. If using a peeler to zest the lemons, use a sharp knife to cut the pieces of zest into fine strips.

3. Arrange the zest on dehydrator trays lined with non-stick sheets or baking parchment. Avoid overcrowding because air needs to circulate around it.

4. Dry at 115°F (46°C) for 4 to 6 hours, rotating the trays a few times during dehydrating. Store in an airtight container at room temperature.

Ginger

Ingredients:

- *Enough ginger to fill your dehydrator*

Dried ginger is a versatile ingredient in any kitchen: it can be used in sweet and savory cooking, ground to a powder for use in spice mixes, or added to different teas for a little kick.

Method:

1. Prepare the ginger by breaking apart the knobs.

2. Peel each knob with a vegetable peeler and cut the pieces into ⅛-inch (3 mm) slices using a sharp knife.

3. Arrange the ginger on the dehydrator trays. Avoid overcrowding because air needs to circulate around it.

4. Dry at 115°F (46°C) for 4 to 8 hours, rotating the trays a few times during dehydrating. Store in an airtight container at room temperature.

△ **Yield:** Varies	△ **Yield:** Varies
⏱ **Prep time:** Variable	⏱ **Prep time:** Variable
〰 **Drying time:** 8–12 hours	〰 **Drying time:** 6–12 hours

Sweet Pepper Powder

Ingredients:

- *Enough sweet peppers to fill your dehydrator*

Making your own sweet pepper powder, when sweet peppers are in season, is a great way to save money and preserve the best produce at season's peak to have on-hand all year round.

Method:

1. Prepare the peppers by cutting them in half lengthways and using a small knife to cut out the stem, seeds and pith.

2. Cut the pepper halves into ¼-inch (5 mm) strips.

3. Arrange the peppers on the dehydrator trays. Avoid overcrowding because air needs to circulate around them.

4. Dry at 115°F (46°C) for 8 to 12 hours, rotating the trays a few times during dehydrating.

5. Once the peppers are completely dry and crisp, place them into a blender or coffee grinder and grind them to a fine powder. Store in an airtight container at room temperature.

Hot Chili Flakes

Ingredients:

- *Enough hot chilies to fill your dehydrator*

Hot chili flakes are a great way to preserve a bumper chili crop, and a wonderfully spicy ingredient to have on hand. Take extra care while grinding/chopping dried chilies that the dust doesn't escape into the air, as it may cause respiratory distress.

Method:

1. Wearing disposable gloves to protect your skin, prepare the chilies by cutting them in half lengthways and using a small knife to cut out the stem, seeds and pith. Leave the seeds in if you prefer hotter flakes.

2. Arrange the chili halves on the dehydrator trays. Avoid overcrowding because air needs to circulate around them.

3. Dry at 115°F (46°C) for 6 to 12 hours, rotating the trays a few times during dehydrating.

4. Once the peppers are completely dry and crisp, place them into a coffee grinder set to coarse, or a mortar and pestle and grind them into flakes. Store in an airtight container at room temperature.

- **Yield:** 1 ½ cups (100 g)
- **Prep time:** 15–20 minutes
- **Drying time:** 8–12 hours

Vegetable Powders

Ingredients:

- *Enough vegetables to fill your dehydrator*

Drying and grinding your own vegetables is a great way to preserve them when in season. These powders can then be added to food and drinks: for extra flavor, and vitamins and minerals, too.

Method:

1. Prepare root vegetables by peeling, removing the ends and using a mandolin set to julienne to cut them into matchsticks.

2. Prepare leafy greens by washing, patting dry with paper towel and removing any woody stalks.

3. Arrange the vegetables on the dehydrator trays. Avoid overcrowding because air needs to circulate around them.

4. Dry at 115°F (46°C) for 4 to 16 hours, rotating the trays a few times during dehydrating.

5. Once the vegetables are completely dry and crisp, place them into a blender or coffee grinder and grind them to a fine powder. Store in an airtight container at room temperature.

Mirepoix

Ingredients:

- *1 lb (450 g) brown onions*
- *8 oz (225 g) carrot*
- *8 oz (225 g) celery*

Mirepoix is the name given for a mix of onion, carrot and celery in specific proportions, that is used as the flavor base for stocks, soups and sauces.

Method:

1. Prepare the onions by removing the ends, cutting them in half and peeling them.

2. Peel the carrots, and remove the ends.

3. Wash the celery, then remove the leaves and ends.

4. Use a sharp knife to dice the vegetables into ½-inch (1 cm) squares.

5. Arrange the vegetables on the dehydrator trays. Avoid overcrowding because air needs to circulate around them.

6. Dry at 115°F (46°C) for 8 to 12 hours, rotating the trays a few times during dehydrating. Store in an airtight container at room temperature.

Chapter Nine:
Breakfast

This chapter provides inspiration for the most important meal of the day. Ranging from tips on how to make your own cereal and granola, to crêpes and pancakes, it has everything you need to enjoy a healthy breakfast with minimal effort.

▲ **Yield:** 5 cups (570 g)	▲ **Yield:** 8 bars
◷ **Prep time:** 45 minutes	◷ **Prep time:** 30 minutes
♨ **Drying time:** 14–19 hours	♨ **Drying time:** 8–12 hours

Classic Granola

Ingredients:

- 1 cup (100 g) raw walnuts, soaked and drained
- 1 cup (150 g) raw almonds, soaked and drained
- 1 cup (170 g) buckwheat groats, soaked and drained
- ½ cup (65 g) raw pepitas, soaked and drained
- ½ cup (65 g) raw sunflower seeds, soaked and drained
- 1 cup (50 g) flaked coconut
- ¼ cup (60 ml) maple syrup
- ¼ cup (60 ml) mango puree
- 1 tsp (2 g) ground cinnamon

This granola is a grain-free, gluten-free and raw twist on a classic breakfast dish.

Method:

1. Roughly chop the walnuts and almonds, then mix all the ingredients together.

2. Allow the flavors to infuse for 30 minutes before spreading the granola evenly onto dehydrator trays lined with non-stick sheets or parchment paper.

3. Dry at 155°F (68°C) for the first 2 to 3 hours, then reduce to 115°F (46°C) for 12 to 16 hours, until the granola is dry and crunchy. Store in an airtight container at room temperature.

Granola Bars

Ingredients:

- 3 medium bananas
- 1 cup (170 g) raw buckwheat, soaked and drained
- 1 cup (135 g) raw pepitas, soaked and drained
- 1 cup (110 g) raw pecans, soaked and drained
- ½ cup (80 g) chia seeds
- ½ cup (100 g) raisins
- ½ cup (50 g) goji berries

Banana and chia seeds bind these bars together, creating a delicious, crunchy bar.

Method:

1. Peel and slice the bananas, then place in a food processor or blender and process until smooth. Add the remaining ingredients and process until the mixture sticks together.

2. On dehydrator trays lined with non-stick sheets or baking parchment, form ½ cupfuls (120 ml) of the mixture into 2-inch (5 cm) by 4-inch (10 cm) bars.

3. Dry at 155°F (68°C) for the first 2 to 3 hours, then reduce the temperature to 115°F (46°C) for 6 to 9 hours, until the bars are dry and firm. Store in an airtight container in the refrigerator.

Raspberry and Coconut Bites

Ingredients:

- ½ cup (45 g) ground flaxseed
- 1 cup (140 g) raw cashews, soaked
- 6 fresh dates, stones removed
- 1 cup (70 g) desiccated coconut
- 1 cup (60 g) shredded coconut
- 2 cups (220 g) fresh raspberries

If fresh raspberries are unavailable for these raspberry and coconut bites, frozen will work just as well. Stirring the raspberries through, rather than blending them, should leave some larger chunks that will give fresh bursts of flavor when you're eating these bites.

Method:

1. Place the ground flaxseed, cashews and dates into the bowl of a food processor and process until the mixture is well combined, but still has some texture.

2. Transfer the mixture to a large mixing bowl and add both types of coconut and the raspberries. Use a spoon to stir the mixture until the coconut and raspberries are mixed through, but some chunks of raspberries remain.

3. Allow the flavors to infuse for 15 minutes before using a large cookie scoop to form the mixture firmly into rounds.

4. Arrange the rounds on the dehydrator trays. Avoid overcrowding because air needs to circulate around them.

5. Dry at 155°F (68°C) for the first 2 to 3 hours of drying, then reduce the temperature to 115°F (46°C) for 10 to 14 hours, rotating the trays a few times during dehydrating, until the bites are firm and dry. Store in an airtight container in the refrigerator.

Orange and Cranberry Bites

⚠ **Yield:** 10–12 bites

🕐 **Prep time:** 45 minutes

〰 **Drying time:** 12–17 hours

Orange and cranberry bites make a great breakfast on the go, or an anytime snack. These bites go well with most dried fruits, so add your favorite in place of cranberries for a new flavor twist.

Ingredients:

- *2 medium oranges*
- *4 fresh dates, deseeded*
- *1 cup (90 g) ground flaxseed*
- *1 cup (130 g) sunflower seeds*
- *1 cup (160 g) dried cranberries*

Method:

1. To prepare the oranges, zest and peel them. Discard the peel.

2. Roughly chop the orange flesh and place it, along with the zest, into the bowl of a food processor.

3. Add the dates, ground flaxseed and sunflower seeds to the food processor and process until the mixture is well combined, but still has some texture.

4. Add the dried cranberries to the orange mixture and pulse a few times to incorporate and roughly chop them.

5. Allow the flavors to infuse for 15 minutes before using a large cookie scoop to form the mixture firmly into rounds.

6. Arrange the rounds on the dehydrator trays. Avoid overcrowding because air needs to circulate around them.

7. Dry at 155°F (68°C) for the first 2 to 3 hours of drying, then reduce the temperature to 115°F (46°C) for 10 to 14 hours, rotating the trays a few times during dehydrating, until the bites are firm and dry. Store in an airtight container in the refrigerator.

Chocolate Crêpes with Bananas

> ⚠ **Yield:** 4–6 crêpes
> 🕐 **Prep time:** 30 minutes
> ♨ **Drying time:** 4–7 hours

A rich, chocolate twist on an old favorite, these chocolate crêpes are easy to make and very indulgent. Here they are served with fresh bananas, but they'd be equally delicious served with fresh berries or cherries, when in season.

Ingredients:

- *6 medium bananas*
- *½ cup (40 g) raw cacao powder*
- *Sliced bananas, to serve*
- *Maple syrup, to serve*

Method:

1. Prepare the bananas by peeling and slicing into 1-inch (2.5 cm) rounds using a sharp knife.

2. Place the bananas and raw cacao powder into the bowl of a food processor or blender and process until the mixture is smooth, about 1 to 2 minutes.

3. On dehydrator trays lined with non-stick sheets or baking parchment, use a spatula to spread ½ cupfuls (120 ml) of the mixture into 6-inch (15 cm) circles.

4. Dry at 155°F (68°C) for the first 2 to 3 hours of drying, then reduce the temperature to 115°F (46°C) for 2 to 4 hours, rotating the trays a few times during dehydrating, until the crêpes are dry and leathery.

5. To serve, place sliced bananas onto each crêpe, drizzle over some maple syrup and fold the crêpes over.

6. Store in an airtight container in the refrigerator.

⚠ Yield: 4–6 crêpes

● Prep time: 30 minutes

♨ Drying time: 4–7 hours

Crêpes with Strawberries and Lemon Cream

These crêpes mean you don't have to miss out on a traditional favorite because of allergies or following a raw food diet.

Ingredients:

For the crêpes:

- 6 medium bananas
- ½ cup (45 g) ground flaxseed
- ½ cup (120 ml) water

For the lemon cream:

- 1 ½ cups (210 g) raw cashews
- 1 lemon
- 3 tbsp (45 ml) maple syrup
- Fresh strawberries, to serve

Method:

1. Peel and slice the bananas into 1-inch (2.5 cm) rounds.

2. Place the bananas, ground flaxseed and water into a food processor or blender and process until smooth, about 1 to 2 minutes.

3. On dehydrator trays lined with non-stick sheets or baking parchment, use a spatula to spread ½ cupfuls (120 ml) of the mixture into 6-inch (15 cm) circles.

4. Dry at 155°F (68°C) for the first 2 to 3 hours, then reduce the temperature to 115°F (46°C) for 2 to 4 hours, rotating the trays a few times during dehydrating, until the crêpes are dry and leathery.

5. Whilst the crêpes are drying, place the cashews into a medium mixing bowl and soak them in enough lightly salted water to cover them, for 4 hours in the refrigerator.

6. Place the cashews into a sieve and rinse well, allow them to drain.

7. Zest and juice the lemon into the bowl of a food processor.

8. Add the cashews and the maple syrup to the lemon and process on high until the mixture is thick, smooth and creamy.

9. Wash, hull and slice the strawberries.

10. To serve, place a generous spoonful of the lemon cream onto each crêpe, add sliced strawberries and fold the crêpes over.

11. Store crêpes and lemon cream separately in airtight containers in the refrigerator.

Chapter Ten:
Entrées

These little dehydrated dishes are a perfect way to begin
a dinner party, or to enjoy as an indulgent treat when you
don't have time to prepare a full meal.

▲ **Yield:** 12 patties	
🕐 **Prep time:** 45 minutes	
〰 **Drying time:** 6–8 hours	

Falafel Patties

Ingredients:

- 2 medium carrots
- 1 small bell pepper
- 1 stalk celery
- ½ cup (65 g) sunflower seeds, soaked and drained
- ½ cup (65 g) pumpkin seeds, soaked and drained
- 1 cup (90 g) ground flaxseed
- ½ cup (65 g) sesame seeds
- ½ cup (20 g) fresh parsley leaves
- 2 tsp (3 g) ground cumin
- 1 tbsp (9 g) garlic powder
- 2 tbsp (30 ml) lemon juice
- 1 tsp (5 g) salt

These falafel patties are not only grain and gluten-free, raw and vegan, they're also legume and nut free, too. Perfect for those who follow a raw or paleo lifestyle. Serve them with salad, or roasted vegetables, or in raw tacos.

Method:

1. Prepare the vegetables by peeling and removing the ends of the carrots, then cutting them into 1-inch (2.5 cm) pieces. Remove and discard the core and seeds of the bell pepper and roughly chop. Slice the celery into 1-inch (2.5 cm) pieces.

2. Place the vegetables into the bowl of a food processor along with the remaining ingredients and process until the mixture is well combined, but still has some texture.

3. Form tablespoonfuls (15 ml) of the mixture into patties using your hands.

4. Arrange the patties on the dehydrator trays. Avoid overcrowding because air needs to circulate around them.

5. Dry at 115°F (46°C) for 6 to 8 hours, rotating the trays a few times during dehydrating, until the patties are dry to touch but still moist inside. Store in an airtight container in the refrigerator.

Taco Shells

⚠ **Yield:** 6–8 shells

🕐 **Prep time:** 15–20 minutes

♨ **Drying time:** 4–7 hours

Dry these taco shells until they are leathery but still pliable enough to be bent, then fill them with your favorite taco fillings: lettuce, tomato, guacamole, falafel patties (page 136), nuts or seeds.

Method:

1. Peel and remove the ends of the onion and carrot, and roughly chop them.

2. Place the onion and carrot into the bowl of a food processor with the remaining ingredients and process until the mixture is smooth and thick.

3. On dehydrator trays lined with non-stick sheets or baking parchment, use a spatula to spread ½ cupfuls (120 ml) of the mixture into 6-inch (15 cm) circles.

4. Dry at 155°F (68°C) for the first 2 to 3 hours of drying, then reduce the temperature to 115°F (46°C) for 2 to 4 hours, flipping the taco shells over after 3 hours and rotating the trays a few times during dehydrating, until the taco shells are dry but still pliable. Store in an airtight container in the refrigerator.

Ingredients:

- *1 small brown onion*
- *1 medium carrot*
- *4 cups (600 g) fresh corn kernels*
- *½ cup (45 g) ground flaxseed*
- *1 tsp (2 g) ground cumin*
- *1 tsp (2 g) paprika*
- *½ tsp (2 g) salt*

Nut and Veggie Loaf

Yield: 6–8 loaves

Prep time: 30–45 minutes

Drying time: 8–13 hours

Ingredients:

- 2 medium carrots
- 2 medium zucchini
- 6 medium mushrooms
- ½ cup (100 g) sundried tomato
- 2 cups (200 g) walnuts, soaked and drained
- 1 cup (90 g) ground flaxseed
- 1 tbsp (9 g) garlic powder
- 2 tbsp (3 g) dried oregano
- 1 tsp (5 g) salt

A raw and vegan twist on classic meat loaf, this nut and veggie loaf is packed full of healthy goodness and flavor. Try blending 1 cup (170 g) of diced tomatoes with ½ cup (100 g) of dried tomatoes and some fresh herbs for a delicious accompaniment.

Method:

1. Prepare the vegetables by peeling the carrots, removing the ends of both the carrots and zucchini and cutting them into 1-inch (2.5 cm) pieces. Remove the stems from the mushrooms and cut the mushrooms into quarters.

2. Place the vegetables into the bowl of a food processor and process until the vegetables are finely chopped.

3. Add the remaining ingredients and continue processing until the mixture is well combined, but still has some texture.

4. Shape cupfuls (240 ml) of the mixture into individual rectangular loaves; approximately 2 inches (5 cm) by 2 inches (5 cm) by 4 inches (10 cm), using your hands or a small loaf pan as a mold.

5. Arrange the loaves on the dehydrator trays. Avoid overcrowding because air needs to circulate around them.

6. Dry at 155°F (68°C) for the first 2 to 3 hours of drying, then reduce the temperature to 115°F (46°C) for 6 to 10 hours, until the nut and veggie loaf is dry on the outside but still moist in the middle. Store in an airtight container in the refrigerator.

Garden Pizza

⚠ **Yield:** Two 11-inch (28 cm) pizzas

🕐 **Prep time:** 30–45 minutes

♨ **Drying time:** 8–13 hours

Why miss out on pizza because you're following a raw food diet or have allergies? This pizza is raw, vegan, and gluten- and grain-free. You can customize the toppings to include all your favorites.

Method:

1. Prepare the zucchini by removing and discarding the ends and cutting into 1-inch (2.5 cm) pieces.

2. Place the zucchini and the remaining base ingredients into the bowl of a food processor and process until the mixture is finely chopped, but not completely smooth.

3. On dehydrator trays lined with non-stick sheets or parchment paper, use a spatula to spread the mixture into two large rounds ¼ inch (5 mm) thick.

4. Dry at 155°F (68°C) for the first 2 to 3 hours of drying, then reduce the temperature to 115°F (46°C) for 6 to 10 hours, flipping the bases and peeling them off the sheets halfway through drying.

5. While the bases are drying, chop the tomatoes and peel and chop the onion for the sauce.

6. Place the onion and tomato into a food processor with the semi-dried tomatoes, chia seeds and basil and process until smooth.

7. Thinly slice the vegetables for the topping, place in a mixing bowl and toss with the apple cider vinegar. Sit in a warm place to soften.

8. To assemble the pizzas, spread the dry bases with the sauce and top with the softened toppings.

9. Store bases, sauce and toppings in separate airtight containers in the refrigerator.

Ingredients:

For the base:
- *2 medium zucchini*
- *2 cups (260 g) sunflower seeds, soaked and drained*
- *1 cup (130 g) golden flaxseed*
- *1 tbsp (1 g) fresh oregano leaves*
- *1 tbsp (3 g) fresh thyme leaves*
- *½ tsp (2 g) salt*

For the sauce:
- *2 medium tomatoes*
- *1 small brown onion*
- *½ cup (100 g) semi-dried tomato*
- *1 tbsp (8 g) chia seeds*
- *8 fresh basil leaves*
- *¼ tsp (1 g) salt*

For the topping:
- *6 medium mushrooms*
- *1 medium bell pepper*
- *2 medium tomatoes*
- *2 tsp (10 ml) apple cider vinegar*

Chapter Eleven:

Desserts

If you have a sweet tooth you are in luck with this chapter, which includes inspirational recipes for indulgent treats that are both delicious and healthy.

Yield: 28–30 cookies

Prep time: 20–25 minutes

Drying time: 12–17 hours

Lemon Cookies

Ingredients:

- *2 cups (280 g) raw cashews, soaked and drained*
- *1½ cups (205 g) raw macadamia nuts*
- *½ cup (80 g) chia seeds*
- *2 tsp (5 g) lemon zest*
- *¼ cup (60 ml) lemon juice*
- *¼ cup (60 ml) maple syrup*

These zingy lemon cookies make the perfect ending to any meal, and the chopped macadamias add an extra element of crunch and texture. The lemon in this recipe could be changed for any citrus fruit with delicious results.

Method:

1. Place the cashews, 1 cup (135 g) of the macadamias, the chia seeds, lemon zest and juice, and maple syrup into the bowl of a food processor and process until the mixture is well combined and sticking together, but still has some texture.

2. Transfer the mixture to a medium mixing bowl. Chop the remaining ½ cup (70 g) of macadamias and stir into the mixture.

3. Form tablespoonfuls (15 ml) of the mixture into rounds using your hands.

4. Arrange the rounds on the dehydrator trays. Avoid overcrowding because air needs to circulate around them.

5. Dry at 155°F (68°C) for the first 2 to 3 hours of drying, then reduce the temperature to 115°F (46°C) for 10 to 14 hours, rotating the trays a few times during dehydrating, until the cookies are firm and dry. Store in an airtight container in the refrigerator.

Yield: 14–18 cookies

Prep time: 30 minutes

Drying time: 10–15 hours

Apricot and Coconut Cookies

Ingredients:

- 2 ¼ cups (245 g) dried apricots
- 2 ½ cups (170 g) desiccated coconut
- 1 cup (140 g) raw cashews, soaked and drained
- ¼ cup (60 ml) maple syrup

Apricots and coconut go together perfectly to create these delicious, chewy cookies. Adding in extra apricot pieces and coconut after blending the mixture gives extra bursts of flavor and texture.

Method:

1. Place 2 cups (195 g) of the dried apricots, 2 cups (140 g) of the desiccated coconut, the cashews, and maple syrup into the bowl of a food processor and process until the mixture is well combined and sticking together, but still has some texture.

2. Chop the remaining ¼ cup (50 g) of dried apricots into pieces and add these and the remaining ½ cup (30 g) of desiccated coconut to the food processor and pulse a few times to combine them.

3. Form two tablespoonfuls (30 ml) of the mixture into a round using your hands; repeat with the remaining mixture.

4. Arrange the rounds on the dehydrator trays. Squash them down if they touch the tray above. Avoid overcrowding because air needs to circulate around them.

5. Dry at 155°F (68°C) for the first 2 to 3 hours of drying, then reduce the temperature to 115°F (46°C) for 8 to 12 hours, rotating the trays a few times during dehydrating, until the cookies are firm and dry. Store in an airtight container in the refrigerator.

Apple Pie Cookies

Yield: 18 cookies

Prep time: 45 minutes

Drying time: 10–15 hours

All the flavors of apple pie, crammed into a delicious cookie. These can also be stored in the freezer for longer storage; simply remove from the freezer 20 minutes before serving.

Method:

1. Peel and core the apples and roughly chop them. Peel the banana and slice into 1-inch (2.5 cm) pieces.

2. Place the apple and bananas into the bowl of a food processor along with the remaining ingredients and process until the mixture is well combined and sticking together, but still has some texture.

3. Allow the flavors to infuse for 15 minutes before using a large cookie scoop to form the mixture firmly into rounds.

4. Arrange the rounds on the dehydrator trays. Avoid overcrowding because air needs to circulate around them.

5. Dry at 155°F (68°C) for the first 2 to 3 hours of drying, then reduce the temperature to 115°F (46°C) for 8 to 12 hours, rotating the trays a few times during dehydrating, until the cookies are firm and dry. Store in an airtight container in the refrigerator.

Ingredients:

- 3 medium apples
- 1 small ripe banana
- 6 fresh dates, stones removed
- 1 cup (150 g) raw almonds, soaked and drained
- 1 cup (140 g) raw cashews, soaked and drained
- 1 cup (90 g) ground flaxseed
- 2 tbsp (30 ml) lemon juice
- 2 tsp (5 g) ground cinnamon
- 2 tsp (5 g) mixed spice

Yield: 16–18 cookies

Prep time: 45 minutes

Drying time: 12–17 hours

Chocolate Shortbread Cookies

These bars have the delicious, crumbly texture of traditional shortbread while being completely raw, gluten and grain free. For a decadent twist, you could stir some dried cherries or chopped macadamias through the mixture before forming it into cookies.

Ingredients:

- *2 cups (140 g) desiccated coconut*
- *1 cup (110 g) raw pecans, soaked and drained*
- *½ cup (120 ml) honey*
- *¼ cup (25 g) ground flaxseed*
- *¼ cup (20 g) raw cacao powder*
- *1 tsp (2 g) vanilla powder*

Method:

1. Place the desiccated coconut and pecans into the bowl of a food processor and process until the mixture resembles breadcrumbs.

2. Add the remaining ingredients to the food processor and process until just coming together.

3. Form two tablespoonfuls (30 ml) of the mixture into a round using your hands, repeat with the remaining mixture.

4. Arrange the rounds on the dehydrator trays. Avoid overcrowding because air needs to circulate around them.

5. Dry at 155°F (68°C) for the first 2 to 3 hours of drying, then reduce the temperature to 115°F (46°C) for 10 to 14 hours, rotating the trays a few times during dehydrating, until the rounds are firm and dry. Store in an airtight container in the refrigerator.

Cashew Caramel Sandwich Cookies

△ **Yield:** 12 cookies

🕐 **Prep time:** 45 minutes

〰 **Drying time:** 10–15 hours

These cashew cookies have a decadent filling made from fresh dates and cashews blended to a smooth, raw caramel. The caramel can take a while to come together, but it is worth the persistence.

Method:

1. To prepare the cookies, place the 2 cups (280 g) of cashews and shredded coconut into the bowl of a food processor and process until the mixture resembles fine breadcrumbs.

2. Add the 8 fresh dates and honey to the food processor and process until the mixture is well combined and sticking together.

3. Form tablespoonfuls (15 ml) of the mixture into balls using your hands.

4. Arrange the balls on the dehydrator trays and flatten them gently using a fork. Avoid overcrowding because air needs to circulate around them.

5. Dry at 155°F (68°C) for the first 2 to 3 hours of drying, then reduce the temperature to 115°F (46°C) for 8 to 12 hours, rotating the trays a few times during dehydrating, until the cookies are firm and dry.

6. While the cookies are drying, prepare the filling by placing all of the filling ingredients into a food processor and processing until the mixture is smooth and sticky and resembles thick caramel.

7. Place teaspoonfuls (5 ml) of the caramel mixture onto one side of half the cookies and top each one with the remaining cookies to make cookie sandwiches.

8. Store in an airtight container in the refrigerator.

Ingredients:

For the cookies:
- 2 ¼ cups (280 g) raw cashews, soaked and drained
- 2 cups (120 g) shredded coconut
- 8 fresh dates, pitted
- 1 tbsp (15 ml) honey

For the caramel filling:
- ½ cup (70 g) raw cashews
- 10 fresh dates, pitted
- ½ tsp (1 g) vanilla powder
- ¼ tsp (1 g) salt

Vanilla Chocolate Bars

Yield: 8 bars

Prep time: 45 minutes

Drying time: 12–17 hours

Ingredients:

- 1 banana
- 1 cup (130 g) raw sunflower seeds
- 2 cups (140 g) raw cashews
- ½ cup (45 g) ground flaxseed
- ¼ cup (60 ml) maple syrup
- ¼ cup (20 g) raw cacao powder
- 1 tsp (2 g) vanilla powder

These vanilla chocolate bars are prepared using cashews and sunflower seeds; soaking the nuts and seeds beforehand makes them softer and easier to blend, bringing the mixture together. Pressing the mixture into a baking pan makes it easier to shape into bars.

Method:

1. Peel the banana and slice it into 1-inch (2.5 cm) pieces.

2. Place the banana into the bowl of a food processor, along with the remaining ingredients and process until the mixture is well combined and sticking together, but still has some texture.

3. Line an 8-inch (20 cm) square pan with baking parchment and press the mixture firmly into the pan.

4. Use the baking parchment to carefully lift the slab out of the pan. Slice the slab into 1-inch (2.5 cm) by-4 inch (10 cm) bars.

5. Arrange the bars on the dehydrator trays. Avoid overcrowding because air needs to circulate around them.

6. Dry at 155°F (68°C) for the first 2 to 3 hours of drying, then reduce the temperature to 115°F (46°C) for 10 to 14 hours, rotating the trays a few times during dehydrating, until the bars are firm and dry. Store in an airtight container in the refrigerator.

Fruit and Nut Energy Bars

△ **Yield:** 16 bars

● **Prep time:** 35 minutes

〰 **Drying time:** 10–15 hours

The combination of nuts and fruit in these bars makes them packed full of energy. They are a fantastic mid-afternoon pick-me-up that's both indulgent and healthy.

Method:

1. Place the nuts and dates into the bowl of a food processor and process until the mixture is well combined and sticking together, but still has some texture.

2. Add the raspberries, goji berries and dried apples to the food processor and pulse a few times to combine and roughly chop the fruit.

3. Line an 8-inch (20 cm) square pan with baking parchment and press the mixture firmly into the pan.

4. Use the baking parchment to carefully lift the slab out of the pan. Slice the slab into 1-inch (2.5 cm) by 4-inch (10 cm) bars.

5. Arrange the bars on the dehydrator trays. Avoid overcrowding because air needs to circulate around them.

6. Dry at 155°F (68°C) for the first 2 to 3 hours of drying, then reduce the temperature to 115°F (46°C) for 8 to 12 hours, rotating the trays a few times during dehydrating, until the bars are firm and dry. Store in an airtight container in the refrigerator.

Ingredients:

- 1 cup (150 g) raw almonds
- ½ cup (50 g) raw walnuts
- 1 cup (110 g) raw pecans
- 10 fresh dates, pitted
- 1 cup (110 g) fresh raspberries
- ½ cup (50 g) goji berries
- ½ cup (50 g) dried apple pieces

<table>
<tr><td>▲</td><td>Yield: 16–18 sandies</td></tr>
<tr><td>◷</td><td>Prep time: 45 minutes</td></tr>
<tr><td>♨</td><td>Drying time: 12–17 hours</td></tr>
</table>

Pecan Sandies

Ingredients:

- *2 cups (220 g) raw pecans, soaked and drained*
- *6 fresh dates, pitted*
- *2 tbsp (30 ml) honey*
- *1 tbsp (6 g) ground chia seed*
- *1 tsp (2 g) vanilla powder*
- *1 tsp (2 g) ground cinnamon*
- *Pecan halves, extra*

This recipe is a raw, gluten and grain-free take on that American classic pecan shortbread, the pecan sandie. These will keep well for a week or so in the refrigerator, or you can pop them into the freezer to keep for longer periods of time.

Method:

1. Place all the ingredients, except the extra pecans, into the bowl of a food processor and process until the mixture is well combined and sticking together, but still has some texture.

2. Form 2 tablespoonfuls (30 ml) of the mixture into a round using your hands; repeat with the remaining mixture.

3. Arrange the rounds on the dehydrator trays. Avoid overcrowding because air needs to circulate around them.

4. Press an extra pecan half into the top of each round.

5. Dry at 155°F (68°C) for the first 2 to 3 hours of drying, then reduce the temperature to 115°F (46°C) for 10 to 14 hours, rotating the trays a few times during dehydrating, until the sandies are firm and dry. Store in an airtight container in the refrigerator.

Maple and Walnut Tarts with Berries

⚠ **Yield:** 24 tarts

🕐 **Prep time:** 45 minutes

♨ **Drying time:** 4–7 hours

These raw tarts are filled with a delicious and tangy raw "jam" and fresh berries, making them a perfect, healthy dessert.

Method:

1. To prepare the tart shells, place the walnuts, cashews, flaxseed, ground chia and maple syrup into the bowl of a food processor and process until the mixture is well combined and sticking together, but still has some texture.

2. Let the mixture sit for 10 minutes to firm up.

3. Line a small tartlet pan with plastic wrap and press tablespoonfuls (15 ml) of the mixture into the tart pan, using your hands to form a shell. Remove the tart shell carefully from the pan by lifting it out using the plastic wrap; repeat with the remaining mixture.

4. Arrange the tart shells carefully on the dehydrator trays. Avoid overcrowding because air needs to circulate around them.

5. Dry at 155°F (68°C) for the first 2 to 3 hours of drying, then reduce the temperature to 115°F (46°C) for 2 to 4 hours, rotating the trays a few times during dehydrating, until the tart shells are dry.

6. While the tart shells are drying, prepare the berries. Place the blueberries, raspberries and chia seeds into the bowl of a food processor and process until smooth. Place the berry mixture into an airtight container in the refrigerator to thicken.

7. Once the tart shells are ready, assemble the tarts by filling each shell with the berry mixture and topping them with extra fresh berries.

8. Store the tart shells and berry filling in separate airtight containers in the refrigerator.

Ingredients:

For the tart shells:
- 2 cups (200 g) raw walnuts, soaked and drained
- 1 cup (140 g) raw cashews, soaked and drained
- ½ cup (45 g) ground flaxseed
- 2 tbsp (12 g) ground chia seed
- ¼ cup (60 ml) maple syrup

For the berry filling:
- 1 cup (130 g) fresh blueberries
- 1 cup (110 g) fresh raspberries
- 2 tbsp (16 g) chia seeds
- Fresh berries, to serve

Chapter Twelve:
Main Meals

This chapter includes delicious meals that you can dry in your dehydrator for use at a later date. Dehydrating cooked meals retains their flavor and makes them lightweight and long lasting. Make your next camping or hiking trip a gourmet affair with the following recipes.

Yield: 4 servings

Prep time: 1 hours 30 minutes

Drying time: 10–18 hours

Bacon and Tomato Pasta Sauce

Ingredients:

- 4 slices bacon
- 2 medium brown onions
- 2 cloves garlic
- 1 small chili
- 1 tbsp (15 ml) olive oil
- 2 tbsp (30 ml) tomato paste
- 2 cups (480 ml) canned diced tomato
- ½ tsp (2 g) salt
- ½ tsp (1 g) ground black pepper
- 2 tbsp (5 g) chopped fresh basil

To rehydrate this pasta sauce, simply place it into a large heatproof pot along with 1 cup (240 ml) of boiling water per cup (240 ml) of dried sauce. Allow the sauce to sit for 1 hour to rehydrate, stirring occasionally and adding more water if necessary. Place the sauce over a medium heat and bring it gently to the boil. While the sauce is rehydrating, cook 1 lb (450 g) of pasta according to package directions, to serve with the sauce.

Method:

1. Slice the bacon into ½-inch (1 cm) pieces.

2. Peel the onions, remove the ends and dice into ½-inch (1 cm) pieces. Peel and finely chop the garlic and finely slice the chili.

3. Place a large, heavy-based frying pan over a medium heat and add the olive oil. Once the pan is hot add the bacon and fry until it is golden and crispy, about 5 to 10 minutes.

4. Add the onion, garlic and chili, and sauté until softened and beginning to color, about 10 minutes.

5. Add the tomato paste, diced tomato, salt and pepper to the pot and bring it to a boil. Reduce the heat to a simmer and cook gently until the sauce has reduced, about 20 minutes.

6. Add the fresh basil, stir it through the sauce and turn off the heat.

7. Spread the sauce thinly onto dehydrator trays lined with non-stick sheets.

8. Dry at 155°F (68°C) for 10 to 18 hours, rotating the trays a few times during drying and using a spoon to break up and move around any large lumps of sauce, so it dries evenly. Store in an airtight container at room temperature.

Hearty Beef Casserole

▲ **Yield:** 4–6 servings

🕐 **Prep time:** 1 hours 30 minutes

♨ **Drying time:** 10–18 hours

This casserole uses lean beef mince in order to shorten the drying time. To rehydrate the beef casserole, simply place it into a large heatproof pot along with 1 cup (240 ml) of boiling water per cup (240 ml) of dried casserole. Allow the casserole to sit for 1 hour to rehydrate, stirring occasionally and adding more water if necessary. Place the casserole over a medium heat and heat it gently until just starting to simmer, then serve.

Method:

1. Prepare the vegetables by peeling the onions and carrots, removing the ends and dicing them into ½-inch (1 cm) pieces. Dice the celery into ½-inch (1 cm) pieces and peel and finely chop the garlic. Peel and dice the potatoes into ½-inch (1 cm) cubes.

2. Place a large, heavy-based pot over a medium heat and add the olive oil. Once hot, add the onion, carrot, celery and garlic and sauté until soft and beginning to color, about 5 to 10 minutes.

3. Add the mince to the pot and sauté until brown, about 10 minutes. Sprinkle the flour over the meat and stir for a further 5 minutes.

4. Add the potatoes, beef stock, dried oregano, salt and pepper to the pot and bring it to a boil. Reduce the heat and simmer gently until the casserole has reduced and the vegetables are cooked, about 45 minutes to 1 hour.

5. Remove the casserole from the heat and spread it thinly onto dehydrator trays lined with non-stick sheets.

6. Dry at 155°F (68°C) for 10 to 18 hours, using a spoon to break up and move around any large lumps of casserole, so it dries evenly. Store in an airtight container at room temperature.

Ingredients:

- *2 medium brown onions*
- *2 medium carrots*
- *1 celery stalk*
- *2 cloves garlic*
- *3 large potatoes*
- *1 tbsp (15 ml) olive oil*
- *2 lb (900 g) lean beef mince*
- *2 tbsp (12 g) plain flour*
- *3 cups (720 ml) beef stock*
- *1 tbsp (3 g) dried oregano*
- *1 tsp (5 g) salt*
- *1 tsp (2 g) ground black pepper*

- **Yield:** 4 servings
- **Prep time:** 1 hour 20 minutes
- **Drying time:** 10–18 hours

Vegetable Curry

Ingredients:

- *2 medium brown onions*
- *2 medium carrots*
- *8 medium mushrooms*
- *1 large eggplant*
- *2 cloves garlic*
- *2 hot chilies*
- *1 large sweet potato*
- *2 tbsp (30 ml) olive oil*
- *1 tbsp (6 g) curry powder*
- *1 tsp (5 g) salt*
- *1 tsp (2 g) ground black pepper*
- *2 tbsp tomato paste*
- *2 cups (480 ml) vegetable stock*

To rehydrate this curry, place 1 cup (240 ml) of boiling water per cup (240 ml) of dried curry into a large heatproof pot. Allow the curry to sit for 1 hour to rehydrate, stirring occasionally and adding more water if necessary. Place the curry over a medium heat and heat it gently until just starting to simmer. Serve with rice, if desired.

Method:

1. Prepare the vegetables by peeling the onions and carrots, removing the ends and dicing them into ½-inch (1 cm) pieces. Dice the mushrooms and eggplant into ½-inch (1 cm) pieces, peel and finely chop the garlic and finely slice the chilies. Peel and dice the sweet potato into ½-inch (1 cm) cubes.

2. Place a large, heavy-based pot over a medium heat and add the olive oil. Once the pot is hot add the onion, carrot, mushroom, eggplant, garlic and chili, and sauté until the vegetables have softened and are just beginning to color, about 5 to 10 minutes.

3. Add the curry powder, salt and pepper, and stir until fragrant, about 2 to 5 minutes.

4. Add the sweet potato, tomato paste and vegetable stock and bring to a boil. Reduce the heat and simmer gently until the curry has reduced and the vegetables are cooked, about 30 to 45 minutes.

5. Remove the curry from the heat and spread it thinly onto dehydrator trays lined with non-stick sheets.

6. Dry at 155°F (68°C) for 10 to 18 hours, rotating the trays a few times during drying and using a spoon to break up and move around any large lumps of curry, so it dries evenly. Store in an airtight container at room temperature.

Mushroom Risotto

Ingredients:

- 1 large brown onion
- 2 cloves garlic
- 5 medium field mushrooms
- 8 small button mushrooms
- 2 tbsp (30 ml) olive oil
- 2 cups (360 g) Arborio rice
- ½ cup (120 ml) white wine
- 4 cups (960 ml) hot vegetable stock
- ½ tsp (2 g) salt, to taste
- ½ tsp (1 g) ground black pepper, to taste
- 2 tbsp (5 g) chopped fresh parsley

To rehydrate this risotto, place it into a large heatproof pot along with 1 cup (240 ml) of boiling water per cup (240 ml) of risotto. Allow the risotto to sit for 1 hour, stirring occasionally and adding more water if necessary. Place over a medium heat and heat it gently until just starting to simmer. Serve with cheese, if desired.

Method:

1. Prepare the vegetables by peeling the onion, removing the ends and dicing it into ½-inch (1 cm) pieces. Peel and finely chop the garlic. Cut the mushrooms in half and slice them into ¼-inch (5 mm) slices.

2. Place a large, heavy-based pot over a medium heat and add the olive oil. Once the pot is hot add the onion and garlic and sauté until they have softened and are beginning to color, about 5 to 10 minutes.

3. Add the mushroom and rice and sauté until the mushroom has softened and the rice is translucent, about 10 minutes.

4. Add the white wine and stir until it has been absorbed. Add the hot vegetable stock to the risotto ½ a cup (120 ml) at a time, stirring until the liquid is absorbed before adding the next lot.

5. Once all the liquid has been added, check the rice is cooked through, adding a little water if necessary. Add the salt and pepper to taste and stir through the parsley.

6. Remove the risotto from the heat and spread it thinly onto dehydrator trays lined with non-stick sheets.

7. Dry at 155°F (68°C) for 10 to 18 hours, rotating the trays a few times and using a spoon to break up any large lumps of risotto, so it dries evenly. Store in an airtight container at room temperature.

Chapter Thirteen:
Pet Treats

Your pet is like a member of the family, so why not treat your furry friend to a special dehydrated snack just like everyone else? You know the ingredients and can keep a watchful eye on the health of your animal.

- ▲ **Yield:** Varies
- ◷ **Prep time:** Variable
- ♨ **Drying time:** 6–8 hours

Liver Treats

Ingredients:

- *Enough liver to fill your dehydrator*

Dogs and cats love liver treats: use them as rewards for training, or just as a special something for your special friend. Use any type of liver you like — beef, chicken, lamb.

Method:

1. Prepare the livers by slicing them into ¼-inch (5 mm) thick slices, then cutting the slices into 2-inch (5 cm) pieces.

2. Arrange the pieces on the dehydrator trays. Avoid overcrowding because air needs to circulate around them.

3. Dry at 155°F (68°C) for 6 to 8 hours, rotating the trays a few times during dehydrating, until the liver is completely dry. Store in an airtight container at room temperature.

Healthy Pet Seed Mix

Yield: 10 seed cakes

Prep time: 20–25 minutes

Drying time: 6–8 hours

Both birds and small furry creatures will love these pet seed treats. Hang them from the trees outside to encourage some feathered friends into your garden, or use them as a special treat for your rabbit or guinea pig.

Ingredients:

- 1 tbsp (12 g) powdered gelatin
- 1 cup (150 g) all-purpose flour
- ¾ cup (180 ml) water
- 2 tbsp (30 ml) honey
- 5 cups (900 g) bird seed mix

Method:

1. Place the gelatin, flour, water and honey into a large mixing bowl and whisk well to combine.

2. Add the bird seed to the bowl and stir until all the bird seed is evenly coated with the gelatin mixture.

3. Place lightly oiled cookie cutters onto dehydrator trays lined with non-stick sheets or parchments paper and fill each cutter with the birdseed mixture, pressing it in firmly with the back of a spoon. Avoid overcrowding because air needs to circulate around them.

4. Use a straw to create a hole in each seed cake, and then carefully remove the cookie cutter.

5. Dry at 125°F (52°C) for 6 to 8 hours, rotating the trays a few times during dehydrating, until the bird seed cakes are completely dry.

6. Thread a piece of string through the hole of each cake and tie it into a loop for hanging. Store in an airtight container at room temperature.

Ingredients:

- *Enough sweet potatoes to fill your dehydrator*

Sweet Potato Treats

Dogs love these chewy sweet potato snacks, and you'll love giving them a treat that's good for them and economical for you. There's no need to peel the sweet potatoes, just give them a good scrub and they're ready to go.

Method:

1. Prepare the sweet potatoes by washing them and slicing them lengthways into ¼-inch (5 mm) slices.

2. Arrange the slices on the dehydrator trays. Avoid overcrowding because air needs to circulate around them.

3. Dry at 125°F (52°C) for 6 to 8 hours, rotating the trays a few times during dehydrating. Store in an airtight container at room temperature.

Puppy Chow

⬚ **Yield:** 2 lb (900 g)

🕐 **Prep time:** 20–30 minutes

♨ **Drying time:** 6–8 hours

Try this delicious, healthy chow on your favorite pup — he'll love it. Use it as a dry food alongside some fresh meat or as training treats for your newest best friend.

Method:

1. Place the carrot, green beans, peas and apple into a large mixing bowl and mix well.

2. In a separate bowl, place the oil, eggs, milk and crumbled bouillon cubes and whisk to combine. Add this to the vegetables and mix well.

3. Add the flour and oats to the wet ingredients and mix until a stiff dough forms.

4. Roll the mixture into 1-inch (2.5 cm) round logs and cut them into 1-inch (2.5 cm) pieces.

5. Arrange the puppy chow on the dehydrator trays. Avoid overcrowding because air needs to circulate around it.

6. Dry at 125°F (52°C) for 6 to 8 hours, rotating the trays a few times during dehydrating, until the chow is completely dry and hard. Store in an airtight container at room temperature.

Ingredients:

- *2 medium carrots, grated*
- *1 cup (135 g) finely chopped green beans*
- *1 cup (135 g) peas*
- *1 medium apple, grated*
- *½ cup (120 ml) oil*
- *2 eggs*
- *1 ½ cups (360 ml) milk*
- *2 bouillon cubes, crumbled*
- *4 cups (600 g) all-purpose flour*
- *3 cups (270 g) quick oats*

▲ **Yield:** Varies

⏱ **Prep time:** Variable

♨ **Drying time:** 6–8 hours

▲ **Yield:** Varies

⏱ **Prep time:** Variable

♨ **Drying time:** 6–8 hours

Salmon Skin Nip

Ingredients:

- *Enough salmon skin to fill your dehydrator*

This is a great way of using up leftover salmon skin from the salmon jerky recipe on page 76. Cats and dogs alike will love this fishy treat, and the fish oils are great for their fur and health.

Method:

1. Prepare the salmon skins by slicing them into 1-inch (2.5 cm) strips, then cutting these into 4-inch (10 cm) lengths.

2. Arrange the strips on the dehydrator trays. Avoid overcrowding because air needs to circulate around them.

3. Dry at 155°F (68°C) for 6 to 8 hours, rotating the trays a few times during dehydrating, until the salmon skin is completely dry and crisp. Store in an airtight container at room temperature.

Chicken Treats

Ingredients:

- *Enough chicken thighs to fill your dehydrator*

Your furry friends will adore you for these tasty treats. Much more economical than store-bought pet treats, and you get the peace of mind of knowing exactly what's in them; just chicken, no nasties.

Method:

1. Prepare the chicken thighs by slicing them into ¼-inch (5 mm) strips.

2. Arrange the strips on the dehydrator trays. Avoid overcrowding because air needs to circulate around them.

3. Dry at 155°F (68°C) for 6 to 8 hours, rotating the trays a few times during dehydrating, until the chicken is completely dry. Store in an airtight container at room temperature.

Chapter Fourteen:

Other Household Uses

Why restrict your use of a dehydrator to finished food products? A dehydrator can be an extremely handy food preparation tool, as well as being wonderful for whipping up some non-food items. This chapter contains some inspirational ideas for the household.

Lemongrass and Ginger Tea

Ingredients:

- 6 stems lemongrass
- 3-inch (7.5 cm) piece ginger

Drying herbs and ingredients for herbal teas is a great way to preserve them for future use when you have an abundance of fresh herbs. The tea combinations are only limited by your imagination, and not just limited to herbs: try adding dried citrus peel or dried fruit for extra zing.

Method:

1. Prepare the lemongrass by washing and cutting it into ¼-inch (5 mm) slices with a sharp knife.

2. Peel the ginger, cut it into quarters lengthways and slice each quarter into ⅛-inch (3 mm) pieces.

3. Arrange the lemongrass and ginger on the dehydrator trays. Avoid overcrowding because air needs to circulate around them.

4. Dry at 115°F (46°C) for 2 to 4 hours, rotating the trays a few times during dehydrating. Store in an airtight container at room temperature.

Yogurt

⚠ **Yield:** 8 cups (1.9 l)

🕐 **Prep time:** 10–15 minutes

♨ **Drying time:** 6–8 hours

Why pay for store-bought yogurt when it's so easy and economical to make your own? Using this recipe as a base, you can then add whatever flavorings you desire: fruit purees and pieces, fruit jellies, nuts, dried fruit; the possibilities are endless.

Ingredients:

- 1 cup (125 g) powdered milk
- 8 cups (1.9 l) fresh milk
- ¼ cup (60 ml) plain, live yogurt

Method:

1. Place the powdered milk and fresh milk into a large saucepan over a medium-high heat, and heat the milk to scalding (just before boiling).

2. Remove the milk from the heat and allow it to cool to 115°F (46°C), checking the temperature with a food thermometer.

3. Once the milk has cooled, add the plain yogurt to the milk and mix well.

4. Pour the milk mixture into the containers you want to store it in, cover them with plastic wrap and place them in the dehydrator.

5. Incubate at 115°F (46°C) for 6 to 8 hours, leaving the yogurt undisturbed for the entire time. Store in the refrigerator.

Drying Pasta

▲ **Yield:** 4–6 servings

🕐 **Prep time:** 1 hour

〰 **Drying time:** 2–4 hours

Ingredients:

- 4 cups (600 g) all-purpose flour
- ½ tsp (2 g) salt
- 6 eggs

There's nothing quite as delicious as homemade pasta and your dehydrator is the key to having it on hand all the time. When you wish to use it, simply cook as you normally would and pair it with your favorite sauce.

Method:

1. Prepare the pasta by placing the flour and salt in a mound on a clean bench. Make a well in the middle of the flour and add the eggs.

2. Use a fork to gradually drag the flour into the egg, mixing gently until a soft dough forms.

3. Once the dough is firm enough to handle, continue to incorporate the flour by kneading the dough with your hands until it forms a smooth, firm, elastic ball.

4. Place the dough into a small mixing bowl and cover it with plastic wrap; allow the dough to rest for 30 minutes.

5. Divide the dough into quarters. Flatten each quarter with your hands and dust them well with flour to prevent sticking.

6. Using a pasta machine, starting at the thickest setting, roll each piece of dough. Then fold the dough pieces into thirds and feed them through the rollers again.

7. Repeat this step three more times, rotating the dough a quarter turn each time.

8. Set the pasta machine to the next lowest setting and roll the sheets through. Continue rolling the sheets through, making the settings one step thinner each time, until your pasta sheets are around ⅟₁₆-inch (1 mm) thick. Continue dusting with flour as needed.

9. Cut the sheets into strips using a spaghetti or fettuccine attachment on the pasta machine, or by hand with a sharp knife. Keep the sheets and strips well dusted with flour.

10. Arrange the pasta in single layers on the dehydrator trays. Avoid overcrowding because air needs to circulate around them.

11. Dry at 135°F (57°C) for 2 to 4 hours, rotating the trays a few times during dehydrating, until the pasta is completely dry. Store in an airtight container at room temperature.

Raising Bread

> **⚠ Yield:** I loaf
> **🕐 Prep time:** 2 hours 45 minutes
> **〰 Drying time:** I hour 15 minutes

Ingredients:

- *I ½ cups (360 ml) warm water*
- *I tbsp (12 g) dried yeast*
- *2 tsp (8 g) granulated sugar*
- *4 cups (600 g) baker's flour*
- *½ tsp (2 g) salt*
- *I tbsp (15 ml) olive oil*

Your dehydrator provides the perfect environment for raising bread, giving you consistent results every time. You can use your dehydrator for any bread recipe, not just the one below.

Method:

1. Set the dehydrator to 115°F (46°C) to allow it to pre-heat. Place a shallow dish of water into the bottom of the dehydrator. Grease a 4-inch (10 cm) by 9-inch (22 cm) loaf pan.

2. Place the warm water, yeast and sugar into a jug and mix well with a fork. Set aside in a warm place until the mixture is frothy, about 10 minutes.

3. Place the flour and salt into a large mixing bowl, make a well in the center and pour in the yeast mixture. Mix well with a spoon until the dough starts to come together, then use your hands to mix it into a soft dough.

4. Turn the dough out onto a lightly floured bench and knead it for 10 to 15 minutes, until the dough is smooth and elastic.

5. Form the dough into a large ball and rub the olive oil over the surface. Place the oiled dough into a large mixing bowl and cover it with plastic wrap.

6. Place the bowl of dough onto a dehydrator tray above the dish of water and allow the dough to rise until it has doubled in size, about 30 to 45 minutes.

7. Remove the dough from the dehydrator and turn it out onto a lightly floured bench. Knead the dough until smooth, and then shape it into a loaf. Place the dough into the loaf pan and put it back into the dehydrator for another 30 minutes.

8. While the loaf is rising, pre-heat the oven to 350°F (180°C).

9. Bake the loaf for 35 to 45 minutes, until the bread is golden and sounds hollow when tapped.

10. Turn the bread out onto a wire rack to cool. Store in an airtight container at room temperature.

Spiced Citrus Potpourri

- **Yield:** 1 bowl
- **Prep time:** 15–20 minutes
- **Drying time:** 8–12 hours

Ingredients:

- 6 oranges
- 2 lemons
- 6 cinnamon sticks
- 2 tbsp (10 g) whole cloves
- 12 star anise

Potpourri is a wonderful way to add a natural, chemical free scent to your home.

Method:

1. Slice the oranges and lemons into ¼-inch (5 mm) rounds and arrange on the dehydrator trays.

2. Dry at 135°F (57°C) for 8 to 12 hours, until the slices are completely dry and crisp.

3. Break each slice roughly into quarters and place in a large mixing bowl. Break the cinnamon sticks into 1-inch (2.5 cm) pieces and add them to the bowl. Add the cloves and star anise and toss the potpourri gently to combine.

4. Store in an airtight container at room temperature.

Lavender and Rose Body Scrub

- **Yield:** 2 ½ cups (600 ml)
- **Prep time:** 15–20 minutes
- **Drying time:** 2–4 hours

Ingredients:

- 12 fresh lavender flowers
- 6 fresh roses
- 2 cups (450 g) granulated sugar
- ¾ cup (180 ml) coconut oil, melted
- 2-3 drops lavender oil
- 2-3 drops rose oil

Why pay for expensive body scrubs when you can so easily make your own? Or package this scrub in an attractive jar as a beautiful and thoughtful gift.

Method:

1. Arrange the flowers on the dehydrator trays. Avoid overcrowding because air needs to circulate.

2. Dry at 115°F (46°C) for 2 to 4 hours, rotating the trays a few times during dehydrating.

3. Place the sugar, coconut oil, lavender oil and rose oil into a large mixing bowl. Mix until well combined.

4. Gently break the dried flowers into pieces and add them to the sugar mixture. Stir gently to combine. Store in an airtight container at room temperature.

Index

Suppliers

Excalibur Dehydrators and Supplies
800-875-4254
www.excaliburdehydrator.com

Léquip
801-383-1920
www.lequip.com

Nesco Dehydrators and Supplies
800-288-4545
www.nesco.com

Presto
1-800-877-0441
www.gopresto.com

Sedona Dehydrators and Supplies
888-254-7336
www.tribest.com

TSM
1-716-824-5814
www.tsmproducts.com

Weston
800-814-4895
www.westonsupply.com

Quintet publishing would also like to thank Fowlers Vacola for kindly supplying an Ultimate Dehydrator and dehydrating equipment for the photo shoot.

About the author

Michelle Keogh is an author, chef, recipe developer and food stylist from Australia. She has over 20 years experience as a chef; running kitchens, restaurants and writing menus. She has spent the last seven years writing recipes and styling food for various publishers and advertising, editorial and commercial clients. She is passionate about all areas of food and cooking and is constantly reading, learning and experimenting.

Michelle has written books for Penguin Books (*Trifle* and *Bundt Cake*), and worked on hundreds of titles for R&R Publications, Hinkler Books and McRae Publishing; food styling, recipe writing and testing. She also develops recipes and styles food for many other clients for commercial use, and in advertising and magazines.

Her personal food interests lean towards wholefood cooking, seasonal and sustainable produce and trying new ingredients, but she also loves the creativity of cake decorating and chocolate making.